Manuel Díaz Rodríguez. Evolution and Dynamics of the Stylist

Scripta Humanistica®

Directed by
BRUNO M. DAMIANI
The Catholic University of America

ADVISORY BOARD

Manuel Díaz Rodríguez
Evolution and Dynamics of the Stylist

Marianna Merritt Matteson

Scripta humanistica

107

Library of Congress Cataloging-in-Publication Data

Matteson, Marianna Merritt.
    Manuel Díaz Rodríguez : evolution and dynamics of the stylist /
Marianna Merritt Matteson.
        p.   cm. -- (Scripta Humanistica ; 107)
    Includes bibliographical references.
    ISBN 1-882528-02-6 : $48.50
    1. Díaz Rodríguez, Manuel, 1871-1927--Style.   I. Title.
II. Series: Scripta Humanistica (Series) ; 107.
PQ8549.D5Z73   1993
863--dc20   93-18340
                                                                CIP

Matteson, Marianna Merritt

    Manuel Díaz Rodríguez. Evolution and Dynamics of the Stylist / Marianna Merritt
    Matteson
        p. cm. — (Scripta Humanistica : v. 107)
    Includes index.
    ISBN 1-882528-02-6 : $45.00

Series: Scripta Humanistica (Series) ; v. 107.

Publisher and Distributor:
SCRIPTA HUMANISTICA
1383 Kersey Lane
Potomac, Maryland 20854 U.S.A.

©Marianna Merritt Matteson
International Standard Book Number 1-882528-02-6

Printed in the United States of America

TABLE OF CONTENTS

Introduction	. . . .	1
Summaries of the Plots	. . . .	6
I. Evocation of Sense Impressions	. . . .	8
Color	. . . .	8
Auditory Sensations	. . . .	18
Olfactory Sensations	. . . .	25
Tactile Sensations	. . . .	27
Sensations of Taste	. . . .	30
II. "Favorite" Words	. . . .	35
III Syntactic Devices	. . . .	52
IV. Imagery	. . . .	75
V. Conclusions	. . . .	85
Tables	. . . .	88
Works Cited	. . . .	96
Additional Bibliography	. . . .	98

ACKNOWLEDGEMENTS

I am indebted to Professor Aníbal Vargas-Barón, my research director at the University of Washington, who first interested me in the study of style. I am also grateful to Washington State University for granting me a professional leave during which this manuscript was completed, and to colleagues for their interest in the project and their support. I have especially appreciated Elwood Hartman's careful reading of the manuscript, and his suggestions.

INTRODUCTION

The relatively brief but brilliant literary career of Manuel Díaz Rodríguez (1871-1927) began in a rather unlikely way, with a wager. Trained as a physician in his native Venezuela, Díaz Rodríguez spent the then obligatory period in Paris and Vienna furthering his medical studies, interrupting these whenever possible with vacation trips throughout Europe. On one of these excursions it is said that he and a companion, seated at a table in a small inn in a remote village in Lombardy, were discussing the merits of a recently published travel book. Díaz Rodríguez, who later revealed that he was an assiduous note-taker on all his travels, remarked that he felt himself capable of writing a better and more successful book. His companion threw down the gauntlet, the notes were transformed into a book, and on Díaz Rodríguez' return to Caracas the same year *Sensaciones de viaje* (1896) was awarded the prestigious prize conferred by the *Academia Venezolana de la Lengua* on the author of the year's best literary work. Díaz Rodríguez abandoned the practice of medicine, to which he never returned, and during the next 14 years devoted himself to literature, establishing himself firmly as one of Venezuela's most highly regarded writers, and particularly as the consummate literary stylist of his generation.

Sensaciones de viaje was followed in quick succession by a collection of short stories (*Confidencias de Psiquis*, 1896), a second travel book (*De mis romerías*, 1898), a second collection of short stories (*Cuentos de color*, 1899), and two novels (*Idolos rotos*, 1901, and *Sangre patricia*, 1902). In 1902 Díaz Rodríguez, in Paris again, was called home by the death of his father and spent the next seven years administering the family estate near Caracas. The collection of philosophical essays later published as *Camino de perfección* (1910) was conceived during this period of retirement.

In 1909 Díaz Rodríguez, in a move many critics are at a loss to explain, turned to politics, and for the remainder of his life served in various capacities in the government of the dictator Juan Vicente Gómez. Two further works were written during this period, a diverse collection of essays, biographical notes and speeches (*Sermones líricos*, 1918), and his third novel, *Peregrina o el pozo encantado* (1922), which included three short stories. A collection of speeches, letters, sketches and verses appeared posthumously (*Entre las colinas en flor*, 1935).

Two quite dissimilar literary movements prevailed in Venezuela, and Latin America, during Díaz Rodríguez' literary career. *Criollismo* (from *criollo*, "native" or "domestic") has been defined by the Venezuelan novelist and critic Rufino Blanco-Fombona as "la pintura, *à outrance*, de las costumbres populares, con los tipos y en el lenguaje del bajo pueblo, lenguaje constelado de provincialismos, muchos de ellos incomprensibles para el lector no venezolano . . . los criollistas [son] enemigos de todo lo exótico" (quoted by Ratcliff 78). Influenced by the great Spanish and French realist-naturalist novelists of the late

1

nineteenth century, *criollistas* were keen observers and recorders of the local scene, focusing not only on customs, people, and language, but on the natural setting as well.

Modernismo was a much more complex movement whose adherents, anything but enemies of the exotic, drew heavily on foreign models, such as the French Parnassians and Symbolists. Critics do not agree on a definition of the movement, but it is safe to say that its distinguishing mark *par excellence* was its meticulous attention to form and style, which included, among a host of techniques, a prevailing preoccupation with color, especially *azul* and *glauco*, and with other sense impressions, innovative uses of vocabulary, the manipulation of syntax to create particular effects, and profound changes in the realm of imagery. Other characteristics on which there is general agreement are an emphasis on individualism, a frequent note of pessimism (both borrowed from the Romantics) and, in the early years of the movement, an element of escapism--of retreat to the "ivory tower"--and an emphasis on the aristocratic. A common theme was the alienation of the artist from a hostile environment. In its later years, specifically beginning around 1898, the year of Spain's disastrous defeat at the hands of the United States, there was a marked refocusing on "lo hispánico," as opposed to "lo exótico," paralleling the concerns of the Spanish *generación del '98*.[1] This new focus was wider than the localism of *criollismo*, and included all of Hispanic America, particularly in calling for a "united front" against the non-Hispanic world, especially the United States.

As should be evident, *criollismo* and *modernismo* are virtually diametrically opposed movements, although elements of both may be present in a work, as indeed many literary works are "hybrid" in terms of belonging to literary movements.

Modernistic characteristics are to be noted in all of Díaz Rodríguez' novels, but of the three works *Sangre patricia* (*Sangre*) is indisputably the purest representative of the movement (Uslar-Pietri 262, Dunham 34, Ratcliff 184). It has been said to be entirely modernistic both in style and content, (Dunham 34, Ratcliff 184), and it is likely that few critics would object to calling it quintessentially modernistic because of the array of modernistic characteristics it displays. The somewhat earlier *Idolos rotos* (*Idolos*) is also considered to be modernistic, (Goić 134, Uslar-Pietri 262), but in it modernistic characteristics tend to appear less frequently and to be used less effectively than in *Sangre*. The much later *Peregrina o el pozo encantado* (*Peregrina*) is usually said to be primarily *criollista* or "Venezuelan," (Díaz Seijas 454, Di Prisco 91, Dunham 71, Picón Salas 150, Uslar-Pietri 263), although it has been recognized that it does not represent a complete break with modernistic tendencies noted in the earlier works.[2] *Peregrina* is a "hybrid" work, in which, moreover, there is a marked tendency to idealize *criollista* elements, for which Díaz Rodríguez has been taken to task by some critics.[3] It does, however, focus on local types and customs, and especially on the details of the natural setting, clear evidence of its *criollista* orientation. The pattern that emerges in the three novels may be said to be one of early modernism in *Idolos* moving to quintessential modernism in *Sangre* and then to attenuated modernism combined with more predominant, if idealized, *criollismo* in *Peregrina*.

The stylistic virtuosity to which Díaz Rodríguez primarily owes his place in Venezuelan letters evolves in a pattern that often reflects this same trajectory; that is, many of the devices characteristic of the author's style that appear in *Idolos* are more prevalent and complex in the more modernistic *Sangre*, and in many cases their use in the predominantly *criollista Peregrina* is considerably attenuated, or disappears. This pattern suggests that Díaz Rodríguez the stylist was most effective when writing in the modernist mode, and indeed most of his work is modernistic in tone.[4]

However, it is also true that in the novels Díaz Rodríguez' style does not conform strictly to this pattern, which might be called an evolution/devolution running parallel to the modernistic emphasis. In fact, it reveals a striking degree of plasticity and dynamism in its adaptation to the three quite different works. In the use of some devices, for example, there is no noticeable change between *Idolos* and *Sangre*, although diminution is to be noted in *Peregrina*, and in a few cases the use of a device remains as frequent and effective in *Peregrina* as in the earlier works. In addition, there are a number of differences between the novels in the application of various stylistic devices. These too can usually be seen to respond in some way to the dissimilar natures of the works, although in a few cases the causative factor appears to be extra-textual.

This study examines several stylistic devices as they appear in the three novels and indicates how, in some cases, they have evolved as Díaz Rodríguez moves from *Idolos* to *Peregrina*, and how, in other cases, they have been adapted to each of the works. The devices studied, although they by no means exhaust all of those characteristic of Díaz Rodríguez' complex style, are 1) the evocation of sense impressions (visual impressions of color, and auditory, olfactory, tactile, and taste sensations), 2) the use of certain "favorite" words, 3) the use of syntactic devices, and 4) the use of imagery.

Determining the relative preponderance in the three works of color words and words evoking olfactory, tactile, and taste sensations, as well as the "favorite" words, lent itself easily to computer searches of the texts, and this method was used to establish frequency data in these areas. In the interest of consistency, the frequency of auditory sensations theoretically should have been determined in this way as well; however, the very large variety of terms employed discouraged the use of the method here.

The frequency of occurrence of terms in the computer generated data was determined by dividing the total number of occurrences of each word by the total number of pages of each novel (see Table I). For example, *azul*, which occurs 34 times in the 206 pages of *Idolos* occurs an average of once on each of 16.50% of the total number of pages. In *Sangre* the frequency of occurrence of *azul* increases markedly,

3

40 times in 90 pages (44.44%), and it is much lower in *Peregrina*, nine times in 101 pages (8.91%). The frequency of occurrence of each of the words is given in Tables II-VI. To ensure that the format of all the novels be the same, data were gathered from the editions of the *Colección Clásicos Venezolanos de la Academia Venezolana de la Lengua* (Volumes I and II, Caracas, 1964), to which all citations refer as well.

Previously published material on syntactic structures in *Idolos* and *Sangre* and imagery and color in *Sangre* has been revised to suit the comparative approach of this study.[5] For those readers who may not be familiar with the novels, brief summaries of the plots are provided.

NOTES

[1] The *generación del '98* refers to a group of Spanish writers and thinkers (Unamuno, Pío Baroja, Azorín, the Machado brothers, Valle Inclán, Benavente, Ganivet, Pérez de Ayala, and Maeztu) united by their profound concern over the problems of their country which had become increasingly evident following the loss of the last vestiges of its once great empire, their attempts to identify the causes of this decline, and their proposal of remedies. The reaction in Hispanic America, often referred to as *mundonovismo, americanismo* or *arielismo* (from José Enrique Rodó's immensely influential *Ariel*, 1900), evidenced not only concern for the problems of Spanish America but a considerable amount of sympathy with the mother country.

[2] The most complete and convincing treatment of this "hybridism" is Crema's essay, but the point is also made by Angarita Arvelo (65-66), Latcham (26), and Ratcliff (187).

[3] Agudo Freytes and Araujo condemn Díaz Rodríguez for his aloofness from reality in *Peregrina*. For the former critic this tendency is tantamount to a failure to fulfill his destiny as the author of the "novela nacional por él concebida y por todos deseada" (47), while Araujo berates him for his failure to recognize beneath the idyllic setting the "drama americano: la explotación del trabajo de hombres, mujeres y niños; el hacinamiento de masas humanas que viven como bestias en el 'repartimiento,' la antigua vivienda de los esclavos; la dramática secuela del alcoholismo embrutecedor, camino por donde la peonada se escapa a la cruenta realidad de su vida para soñar otra mejor" (154). Castro notes that *Peregrina* "abandona toda influencia realista para captar una naturaleza que es fijada en descripciones poéticas y donde los conflictos sociales o meramente humanos son falsificados hasta hacerlos irreconocibles" (16). More charitably, Julio Planchart has called it "una linda novela bucólica" (quoted by Ratcliff, 186). Whatever Díaz Rodríguez' failings in this regard may be, the distancing is clear throughout the novel.

4

4 Notable exceptions, besides *Peregrina*, are the three short stories published with it, "Música bárbara," "Egloga de verano," and "Las ovejas y las rosas del Padre Serafín," which are quite realistic, with elements of naturalism.

5 Matteson, Marianna M., "Imagery in Díaz Rodríguez' *Sangre patricia*," *Hispania* 56 (1973): 1014-20; "Motivos sintácticos en *Sangre patricia*," *Explicación de Textos Literarios* II.2 (1974): 131-36; Matteson, Marianna Merritt, "Syntactic Patterns in Díaz Rodríguez' *Idolos rotos*," *Selecta* 5 (1984): 116-21; "The Symbolic Use of Color in Díaz Rodríguez' *Sangre patricia*," *Hispania* 68 (1985): 35-43.

SUMMARIES OF THE PLOTS

Idolos rotos

Three interrelated themes form the plot of *Idolos*: 1) the frustrated artistic career of the protagonist, 2) bitter, often satirical, criticism of the socio-political *milieu* of Venezuela, which is seen as the principal cause of his artistic failure, and 3) his disastrous affair with a woman totally unsympathetic with his artistic ambitions, which becomes symbolic of his failure.

Alberto Soria is introduced to the reader as he returns to Caracas from Paris, where he had gone to study engineering, but where, like his creator, he had turned to art, in his case sculpture. Having won a prize in Paris for his first work, he anticipates attaining the same recognition in his homeland, but the *milieu* of Caracas proves antagonistic from the beginning. Criticism appears early and continues throughout. Upper-class society, from which Alberto quickly recognizes his isolation, is portrayed as selfish and superficial, and politicians as self-serving, incompetent, and totally hostile to the notions of beauty and art. In addition, the members of Alberto's family, beset with a number of problems of their own, offer him little support.

Alberto manages to cope initially, sustained by his love for a childhood friend, María Almeida, his work, and the support of a small circle of like-minded friends, a "ghetto" of intellectuals, who together develop plans for the regeneration of the country through the dissemination of culture. All of these are doomed. Alberto's love for María wanes, he becomes obsessed with the voluptuous Teresa Farías, and the destructive nature of this relationship leads him to neglect his work. The plans for cultural regeneration are thwarted by a revolution, during which Alberto's statues are desecrated and destroyed by brutish soldiers under the command of an equally brutish general. All of his dreams--of art, love, and the regeneration of his country--in ruins as well, Alberto decides to emigrate, and the novel ends on an extremely pessimistic note: FINIS PATRIAE.

Sangre patricia

The plot of *Sangre* has been called weak, but although it is superficially simple, the novel abounds with symbolism and in this sense its structure is quite complex. It opens as Belén Montenegro embarks on a voyage to join the protagonist in France; they have recently been married by proxy in Caracas. On the fifth day of the voyage Belén, who has enchanted and mystified her fellow passengers with her beauty, dies unexpectedly and is buried at sea. There follows a flashback introducing the protagonist, Tulio Arcos, scion of an aristocratic family and another social misfit. Tulio is a typical *abuliac*; that is, he suffers from lack of will, specifically in his case the ability to decide whether he wishes to devote himself to the profession of arms or that of letters. He finally opts for the former, joins a revolutionary band, is captured, and exiled to France where we find him as the novel begins.

On learning of Belén's death, Tulio reacts by developing a psychological ailment which manifests itself as a dream state in which he imagines that he descends to the bottom of the sea where he joins his bride. It is revealed that the dream, which at first seems to accost him randomly, is caused by the suggestive power of the color green, or of water, which interact in a complex manner to remind him of Belén's green eyes and the sea, and lead to the submarine fantasy. The dream becomes so persistent that it dominates him almost completely, although it is interrupted briefly when he responds to a call from compatriots who beg him to return to Venezuela to participate in another uprising. On the return voyage he is accosted by another related fantasy: he imagines that a mermaid seduces him nightly in his cabin. At the end of the novel he imagines he hears her calling him from the sea, and he plunges overboard to join her.

Peregrina

The characters of *Peregrina* are the peasants who work an *hacienda* in the countryside near Caracas. Although many characters are introduced, and we observe various aspects of their daily life, attention is focused on three of them--the half-brothers Amaro and Bruno, and the girl they both love, Peregrina. The brothers are quite unalike; Amaro is shy and steady, Bruno extroverted and mercurial.

Bruno manages to seduce Peregrina and they begin to meet secretly at night while Bruno, to divert attention from any suspicions of their clandestine activity among the other inhabitants of the compound, plays on their superstition by inventing a series of seemingly ghostly phenomena. The affair continues, interrupted by Bruno's forays into the nearby mountain, the Avila, to gather orchids, which he sells in Caracas. Peregrina becomes increasingly concerned about the possible consequences of their affair, and on realizing that she is indeed pregnant begins to pressure Bruno to marry her. He is evasive. On one of his trips to the capital he has a strange encounter with a woman who insists on keeping her identity secret, and his estrangement from Peregrina deepens. Meanwhile, Peregrina's father determines that Bruno must marry her and Amaro is dispatched to deal with his brother. Bruno, now much more interested in his mystery woman than in settling down with Peregrina, suggests that Amaro marry her himself, provoking an attack in which Amaro nearly kills his brother. Bruno, however, escapes. Peregrina, at first confident he will return, becomes increasingly depressed as his absence lengthens. After a heavy rainfall Amaro and another *campesino* see her walking beside a swollen stream, and she falls into it, whether accidentally or deliberately is not clear. Rescued by the two men, she is taken to her father's house, where she falls ill and loses the baby. Bruno, on hearing of her illness, finally returns and offers to marry her. It is, of course, too late. Peregrina dies and the inconstant Bruno disappears again the same night.

7

CHAPTER I

EVOCATION OF SENSE IMPRESSIONS

One of the most prevalent characteristics of modernistic prose and poetry, an emphasis on sense impressions, is quite evident in Díaz Rodríguez' three novels. Particularly common are impressions of color, and various kinds of auditory sensations, but there are also evocations of odors, various tactile sensations, and a few allusions to taste.

Color

The number of color words or words suggestive of colors (such as *sangre* or *nieve* or names of precious stones or flowers) used in the novels is quite large, but in general they fall into the following generic groups: red, white, green, blue, yellow, black, purple, gray, brown, silver, and orange (extremely rare). Red, white, green, blue, yellow, and black are clearly the preferred colors in all the novels, the others appearing less frequently, or not at all, but colors do not appear with the same degree of frequency, nor are color allusions used for the same purpose in all the works. The distribution of generic colors is revealing, as is that of many of the specific terms, as one compares the early modernistic *Idolos*, the quintessential modernistic *Sangre*, and the primarily *criollista Peregrina* (see Table II).

In *Sangre* generic green, red, white, and blue, which occur with nearly equal frequency, clearly predominate over the other colors (some of which do not appear). Since, as will be seen, these colors are often used symbolically and linked to structural elements in the novel, their preponderance might be expected. It will also be noted that green, white, and blue occur with considerably greater frequency in *Sangre* than in the other novels, indicating their more strategic function in that novel.

Red clearly predominates in *Idolos*, where it will also be seen to be used symbolically and linked to structure, and in *Peregrina*, in which symbolic associations are minimal but where it figures prominently as a descriptive element.

The frequency of generic yellow and purple is much greater in the *criollista Peregrina*, with its emphasis on the natural setting (purple does not appear in *Sangre* and is rare in *Idolos*), and brown and silver, which do not occur in *Sangre*, are also more common in *Peregrina* than in *Idolos*. The expanded palette of *Peregrina* also includes one evocation of orange, which is not found in the earlier novels. Although *Peregrina* retains many modernistic characteristics, the low frequency of blue, the modernists' favorite, is an indication of the shift to a more *criollista* orientation.

There is a more noticeable tendency in *Sangre* than in the other novels to employ specific color words that are more "poetic" than simply descriptive. *Armiño, cándido, candidez, glauco,* and *áureo* appear more frequently than in the other works, and *cárdeno* and *róseo* appear only in *Sangre.* On the other hand, the palette of *Peregrina* includes a number of specific descriptive terms not found in the other works *flamígero, rojeante, rojez, rojizo, ámbar, amarilleado, amarillito, azabache, ébano, amatista, morado,* and *cobrizo.* The word *sangre* appears very frequently in *Sangre* in a non-color suggestive function, as the title suggests it might, but the term is also used to evoke the color red more frequently than in the other novels.[1]

Not surprisingly, the total frequency of all color words is significantly higher in *Sangre* than in *Idolos* or *Peregrina*; that it is higher in *Peregrina* than in *Idolos* is not surprising either, in view of the marked emphasis on the natural setting in *Peregrina.*

As Díaz Rodríguez moves from *Idolos* to *Peregrina* there are further differences between the novels in the application of specific stylistic devices the relative prevalence of figurative language in allusions to color, the evocation of wide ranges of color or subtle shades of specific colors, the symbolic use of some colors, and the manner in which symbolic colors are integrated into structural elements.

In *Idolos* color words, or words suggesting color, are often used in a purely descriptive sense, employing non-metaphoric language, as when Alberto contemplates from his window a "paisaje, a lo lejos velado ligeramente de azul" (220), or in the following reference to his reactions to the beauty of the countryside: " . . . de los verdes cafetales vecinos, ya salpicados de rojo gracias a la madurez de los frutos; de los montes; del cielo azul, pocas veces pálido; de todo el valle parecía fluir, buscando el alma de Alberto, una como agua muy pura" (246).

Quite frequently, however, allusions to color employ metaphoric language. The use of *rosas* to describe the color of the sky at sunset is an apparent favorite of Díaz Rodríguez, occurring several times. On Alberto's first excursion in Caracas shortly after his return from Paris, he enjoys the view of the sunset from "El Calvario:"

> Cuando Alberto se dispuso a bajar del Calvario hacía tiempo que las rosas del largo crepúsculo de septiembre se deshojaban en el cielo occiduo. Mientras él bajaba, aproximándose a la ciudad, seguían deshojándose las rosas de luz, ya no solamente en el cielo occiduo, sino en todos los puntos del cielo. Y las rosas deshojadas caían sobre el Avila, sobre los techos de las casas, sobre las torres de los templos, en las calles de la ciudad, e inflamaban la atmósfera. (202)

9

As the light fades, Díaz Rodríguez notes that "morían las últimas rosas diáfanas" (203), and as Alberto ends his excursion he "veía de nuevo, sobre el desaseo de las calles, deshojarse las infinitas rosas del crepúsculo" (204). At another point Romero, one of Alberto's "camaradas de 'ghetto,'" lamenting the political situation in Venezuela, "terminó por desear que el Bolívar del monumento de la plaza y su caballo de bronce desaparecieran de improviso, una tarde, entre la lluvia de rosas del crepúsculo, en un relámpago, para que no honrasen más con su gloriosa pesadumbre aquel pedazo de tierra maldito" (285), and another "camarada," Emazábel, uses the same association when he refers to the dust of Caracas' streets that floats in the air "mientras el cielo vuelca sobre la ciudad indiferente sus púrpuras y sus rosas" (289).

There is some tendency in *Idolos* to evoke a quite wide range of colors in a single passage. This is evident in another description of sunsets, in which allusions to precious stones and flowers also contribute to the intense sensation of color and light:

> Tan escrupulosa y consagrada atención Alberto ponía en seguir los cambios de la luz y las diversas tintas de las aguas y del cielo, que algunos crepúsculos, con sus mas imperceptibles pinceladas, quedábansele hasta mucho tiempo después resplandeciendo en la memoria. Ya era un ocaso en que un largo nubarrón plomizo, como densa faja de brumas, ocupaba el horizonte; por sobre la nube, un haz de tintas pálidas, que se desmayaban y morían como pétalos de flores enfermas; debajo, entre la nube y las aguas del mar, una tenue raya color de fuego, como hecha con un pincel fino y primoroso; y el vientre mismo de la nube horadado, en el sentido de su longitud, en tres puntos diferentes, de los cuales, como de otros tantos respiraderos de una fragua, saltaban a la mar sendos fúlgidos chorros de topacios derretidos. Ya era otro crepúsculo admirado desde el puentecito del establecimiento de baños; detrás del pueblo, de la más alta cumbre del monte, se desprendía, subiendo en los aires y avanzando a la vez hacia el mar, un blanco jirón de niebla; . . . en el cielo de Occidente, dos lagos: uno de oro con bordes azules, el otro de fuego con orillas de ópalo; y entre esos dos lagos y el jirón de niebla que subía de la montaña, una gran zona celeste, clara y profunda, en cuyo fondo chispeaba el primer lucero de la noche como diamante solitario prendido en el velo azul de una virgen. (325)

There is also to be noted some tendency to evoke subtler shades of basic colors--*tonos amarillos y rosados* (173), *rojo oscuro* (204), *rubio suave* (241), *blanco mate* (337), *oro pálido* (226), *ojos medio verdes, medio azules* (208), *gris casi negro* (204), *rubí casi negro* (173), *blancura mate* (342), *áureo y mate color de canela* (267)--but these do not occur frequently.

10

On several occasions color words are used symbolically. As it did for the modernists, *azul* may symbolize beauty, love, the ideal, or the infinite. Describing a book brought back from Paris, Alberto notes that it "puede caber en el hueco de una mano chiquitina. Y con toda su belleza, en la belleza de la mano, sería como una gota de agua con todos los esplendores del Azul posada sobre un pétalo" (198). Referring to Alberto's earlier adolescent attraction to María Almeida, Díaz Rodríguez notes that it "no había hecho sino rozarle con su ala azul y huir muy lejos" (192), and when his more mature attraction has developed to the point that he recognizes it as love, Alberto is moved to invoke a veritable arsenal of modernistic color connotations to express his perception of various kinds of love, María's being associated with blue:

> Hay gentes que no ven el color sino en las cosas. No lo alcanzan a ver en las almas. También en las almas hay color, María. Y tu amor es azul . . . Hay mujeres cuyo amor descolora . . . Es un amor egoísta y malo. Hay otras mujeres cuyo amor es fuego y púrpura: tiñe de rojo las almas. Las almas encendidas en ese amor ven el mundo como a través de un velo de sangre; adquieren por un momento sobrehumana esplendidez, y pronto se consumen como aristas en la hoguera. Es pérfido ese amor: da a las almas una gran belleza efímera, y las destruye en cambio. Hay otras cuyo amor es azul, y ese no descolora ni destruye; antes pone el infinito en un alma. El azul ama lo infinito, y el infinito ama lo azul y se complace en tomar apariencias azules. El cielo es azul, María. (249)

Much more frequent are symbolic uses of red, which is often associated with passion--of love or of war. As Alberto notes in the passage cited above, there are women, whose love he associates with red, who destroy. This is, of course, the kind of destructive passion that will characterize his later affair with Teresa Farías. As his irrational jealousy of her past begins to sour his relationship with María, red is juxtaposed with white, associated with the notion of purity, emphasizing his loss of faith in the idyllic nature of this relationship and foreshadowing the nature of his relationship with Teresa: "Alberto vio las rosas, hasta entonces blancas de su idilio, comenzar a teñirse de púrpura" (303).

Red is frequently associated with the passion-based relationship he forms with Teresa, and with the revolution and its disastrous implications for his artistic career, which together comprise the content of the fourth and final part of the novel. As the section opens, with Alberto awaiting the arrival of Teresa for an assignation at his studio, a figurative parallel, described in terms of heat and redness, is drawn between the parched earth of the dry season and the feverish passion he feels for her:

> La tierra tenía fiebre. El calor de la fiebre se alzaba por todas partes de la tierra sitibunda, y también por todas partes el rubor de la fiebre subía en llamaradas violentas a la cima de los

11

bucares, a lo alto de las marías, a las copas de las acacias, que se desgajaban de flores. No se veía sobre los árboles, en ninguna parte de la ciudad ni en sus contornos, sino florescencias purpúreas, reveladoras del incendio que abrasaba las entrañas de la tierra. Desde la ventana del taller se divisaba a lo lejos, por sobre las tapias de un corral, una maría empavesada de púrpura . . . También él, como la tierra, tenía fiebre . . . (322)

The allusions to heat and redness are further extended, first to the flames of the stubble-clearing *roza* that engulf the surrounding countryside, which become visible after night has enveloped the sight of the figuratively flaming foliage, and then to the country itself, in which revolution is viewed as inevitable:

Mientras Alberto admiraba el incendio de la roza, en su espíritu se abría la flor de un símbolo. Y en el símbolo creyó ver la explicación de la última época de su vida, creyó ver la explicación de la vida alborotada de las gentes de su país y creyó penetrar el secreto del alma de aquellas comarcas, triste, ardorosa y enferma. Las purpúreas coronas de llamas de la roza eran las únicas dignas del dios de aquellas comarcas, un dios indígena semibárbaro y guerrero, cruel y voluptuoso, un dios que fuera al mismo tiempo el dios de la Voluptuosidad, la Codicia y la Sangre. (359)

Red is juxtaposed with white to refer to the somewhat schizoid personality of Teresa, who responds with equal fervor to the thrills of carnal passion and those of repentance: "En Teresa andaban siempre juntos la plegaria y el deseo. Nacían de su corazón como dos flores gemelas de una planta que diese a la vez flores blanquísimas y flores de púrpura" (336). On a more purely descriptive, but still suggestive level, the *santuario de amor* adjoining Alberto's studio, site of his trysts with Teresa, is closed off by a "cortina de damasco purpúreo" (345, 365).

The other frequently occurring colors--green, yellow, and black--as well as the occasional gray, purple, brown, or silver, are usually used in a purely descriptive, non-metaphoric sense, as in "rocas negruzcas y tierra árida, color de ocre, de tonos amarillos y rosados, a trechos cubierta de raros manchones de verdura," (173). There is an occasional metaphor, as in the "mezcla de oro y canela" (220) of the type of native female beauty Alberto wishes to capture in clay, or the "gualda túnica de los araguaneyes florecidos," (175), but there is no symbolic use of these colors.

Colors in *Sangre* may have, as in *Idolos*, a purely descriptive or decorative function and be evoked by means of non-metaphoric language, as when Tulio contempla "la línea verde y azul de la costa" (74) or when the sea is described as "roja porque la tiñen de carmín las purpúreas eritreas" (73), but occurring with considerable more frequency than in *Idolos* is the use of metaphoric language in the evocation of colors, especially blue. This is to be noted, for example, in the wide array of color-based metaphors used to describe the sea: *boca insaciable y azul* (9), *sonrisa del agua azul* (9), *camino azul* (25, 26), *desierto azul* (27), *noche azul del océano* (27), *copa azul del Mediterráneo* (70), *sonrisa azul del agua* (72), *manto azul del Mediterráneo* (76), *tálamo azul de las peces* (85), *azules praderas* (87), *polvo de zafiros* (25), *arcas de zafiro* (33), *zafiro del mar* (70), *espejo de zafiro* (70), *alma de zafiro* (73), *sepultura glauca* (26), *sonrisa glauca* (70), and *glauco señuelo de la onda* (78). The very suggestive and modernistic "rosa de aire azul" (81) that refers to shipboard romances is another example, which is also representative of the type of imagery discussed in chapter IV.

The technique noted in *Idolos* of evoking a gamut of color is also intensified in *Sangre*, especially in the passages describing the fantastic landscape of Tulio's dream world. Extended descriptions, in which there is also considerable emphasis on flowers and precious stones, occur on pp. 38 and 75-76; the following is representative of these:

> De esta suerte llegó a donde se alzaba de la tierra, penetrando con impetuosidad en las aguas, como un deseo irresistible, una montaña purpúrea. Tal vez una montaña de coral; tal vez alguna inmensa columna de lava salida de las entrañas de la tierra, para cuajarse, en la gloria de su color, al húmedo beso de las linfas. En su mayor altura esplendía algo muy blanco, de extrema candidez, como un gran lirio abierto sobre una montaña de rosas. A muy corta distancia de donde blanqueaba esa cándida flor gigantesca, se dilataron, con el asombro del prodigio, los ojos de Tulio. En el seno de la blancura chispearon, como vivas turquesas, dos ojos glaucos: los glaucos ojos de Belén; se agitaron, como pétalos, dos labios por cuya curva de flor se deslizó el alba de una sonrisa: la sonrisa de Belén; y, en el gran lirio abierto sobre una montaña de rosas, Tulio reconoció a Belén . . . (38)

The inclination to evoke subtler shades of basic colors that was evident to some degree in *Idolos* is greatly increased in the case of green in *Sangre*. Green color words are quite often modified by adjectives or used in phrases which suggest some shading: *claro verde y luminoso* (28), *verde claro* (43), *verde turbio* (43), *pálidos reflejos glaucos* (45), *agua verde obscura* (57), *los más dulces y desvaídos colores glaucos* (67), *tonos glaucos* (67), *matices claros del verde* (67), *matices glaucos* (68), *los verdes más pálidos* (68), *los más desvaídos colores verdes* (70, 74-75). Subtler shades of colors other than green are less common than in *Idolos*, although some do occur: *sangre de los más pálidos corales rosas* (6), *cálido azul intenso* (8), *azul turquí* (8), *fogosa púrpura* (78).

The use of colors with a symbolic function is much more prominent in *Sangre* than in *Idolos* and contributes substantially to the coherence of the plot and to the comprehensibility of the principal characters, particularly Tulio Arcos.[2]

13

Red may be associated with physical passion, as it is in *Idolos*. This is to be noted in the comparison of the fantastic *montaña de púrpura* with *un deseo irresistible* in the passage cited above, and in two of the other passages describing the landscape of the dream. In one of these Tulio is actually contemplating boats on the Adriatic as he experiences the dream, and the reference is to "velas de púrpura, tales como inquietas llamas de amor" (75). In the other passage "magnolias de púrpura . . . se descogían y encogían con movimiento voraz de bocas ávidas" (76). These links, however, are few, and they lack the overt sensuality and the vehemence that characterize the association in *Idolos*. In *Sangre* this association is, in fact, a faint echo of that found in the earlier novel.

Red is associated primarily, as it sometimes is in *Idolos*, with the notion of war, but in *Sangre* this connection is extended to include the notion of heroism in war, and in this function red is often juxtaposed with white, which here symbolizes beauty or the arts, the other facet of Tulio's inner conflict:

> Y el ideal, en aquella época obscura, tampoco florecería en cándidas imágenes de belleza, como un jazmín; daría flores como el rosal, en un incendio de púrpura. No rompería con timidez bajo la pluma, en cada palabra, como un azahar o una violeta; surgiría en el extremo de la espada con el triunfo de la rosa. La vara del ideal había de ser una limpia hoja de acero; su flor, una rosa de sangre. . . . La guerra forma pueblos, constituye naciones, hace la unidad y grandeza de las razas. . . . Como hermanas gemelas de su pródigo vientre nacen la gloria del capitán y la gloria del artista: el laurel tinto en sangre y la obra de arte vestida de candidez impoluta. (21)

The symbolic function of blue overlaps that of white to a considerable degree; together these colors may be said to symbolize the vague and subtle notions of beauty, art, love, the ideal, and the mystical. White and blue are associated with two of Tulio's forbears who did not participate in the warrior tradition that is symbolized by red--an artist and a nun, who is a kind of mystic. In the description of the painter neither color is explicitly mentioned, but blue is suggested by the word *cielo* and white by *azahares* and *granizo*:

> Nació a la belleza bajo el cielo granadino. . . . se bañó en la lluvia de azahares que, de los naranjos ribereños del Guadalquivir, baja como lluvia de fragante granizo a perfumar la tierra; . . . y enfermó de la tristeza de su voluptuosidad, hasta morir en ese mismo paisaje, soñando sueños imposibles como los de un califa insano y voluptuoso. (12-13)

The description of the nun is rich in words suggesting whiteness, and *cielo* again suggests blue:

14

Pasó por entre las meditaciones del convento como una aparecida blanca y dulce. . . . Era un sueño que pasaba . . . Desde muy pronto, la descarnó el ayuno, la maltrató el cilicio, y el fresco lirio de su belleza fue poco a poco enrojeciéndose, hasta ser una sangrienta rosa expiatoria. La sangre de su crucifixión estaba oculta bajo muy cándidas tocas monjiles. Pero si sus tocas monjiles eran cándidas, aun mas cándidas eran las palomas que volaban dentro de su corazón como en un cielo muy puro. (13) [3]

Also significant to the chromatic symbolism of the novel is the association of both artist and mystic with the concept of *sueño* and the linking of this concept with blue to describe their lives: ". . . apenas hubo dos que penetraron el secreto de la miel escondida en la copa insondable y azul del ensueño" (12). In the contexts being considered, the element *sueño* (or *ensueño*) *azul* may probably be taken to mean "dream" in the sense of "ideal." This interpretation is supported by the fact that *azul* appears on other occasions linked to the concept of *sueño* in contexts in which they clearly refer to some sort of ideal; for example, the "amor tranquilo y sano suspendido sobre el sueño azul de los pozos" (53) imagined by those aboard ship when they perceive land, and the "complicada urdimbre de sueños vagos y azules" (78) woven by those fellow passengers of Tulio's who are of poetic nature. Finally, near the end of the novel, *sueño* is linked to *azul* and blue contrasted with red in an image which conveys very forcibly the notion that Tulio's imaginary idyll with Belén has been interrupted by a call to arms: "Y sobre el diáfano azul del sueño, abrió, como un alba sobre el mar, una rosa de sangre" (77).

Green is associated with Belén, the sea, and with Tulio's psychological state. There is considerable emphasis on Belén's green eyes, which, besides her hair and general beauty, are the only physical features we really "see." She, in turn, is associated with the sea, since by virtue of her almost supernatural beauty, her mysterious death, and her burial at sea, she shares with it the element of mystery. Her fellow passengers note this early in the novel, seeing in her beauty "algo del color, un poco de la sal y mucho del misterio de los mares" (6), and Tulio asks himself shortly after learning of her death, "¿Aquella muerte no revelaba entre la existencia del mar y el destino de Belén una perfecta armonía profunda? Belén tenía los ojos como glaucos remansos limpísimos . . ." (33). Tulio himself "se encontró de improviso en una obscuridad preñada de misterio. El misterio lo aumentaba la circunstancia de aquella muerte en plena juventud y en plena mar" (33).

As Tulio's illness progresses, he becomes highly susceptible to the visual impact of shades of green, which exert a sort of hypnotic power over him, inducing the dream state. But the state is actually induced because the sight of green things reminds him of the color of the sea and of Belen's eyes:

El sueño lo asaltaba en la calle, en el café, en todas partes, como un encantamiento súbito. En apariencia espontáneo, se lo sugerían en realidad muchas cosas, como ciertas esmeraldas entrevistas en el escaparate del joyero, el follaje nuevo de los árboles, la turba linfa del ajenjo y de otros licores, la onda glauca del río y cuantas cosas le recordaban, por su color, las aguas del océano y los ojos de la amada. (67)

I have suggested elsewhere that the sea, and by extension Belén and the color green, suggest to Tulio the ultimate mystery of the essence of things, which is Díaz Rodríguez' definition of mysticism in literature, and that Tulio's retreat into his private *sueño verde* and his ultimate suicide may be viewed as an effort to penetrate this mystery.[4] This affords to green a vital and pervasive function in the novel, since it is intimately associated with the development and ultimate outcome of the plot.

White, which is associated with the painter and the nun, is also associated with the composer and musicologist Alejandro Martí, perhaps the most important secondary figure in the novel, in whom the artistic and the mystical are fused: "Blanda luz mística bañó su fe y su arte, y la unión del arte con la fe completó la unión, ya realizada en él, del arte con la vida" (51). Martí's life is compared to a "flor blanca y sonora" (49) and his virtue to "seda cándida y firme" (49).

White is sometimes contrasted with black, which has negative connotations, in passages in which Martí appears. Martí had at one point contemplated suicide, and in two passages referring to this crisis white and black are contrasted:

Por vez primera el desaliento, como uno de esos negros pulgones robadores de miel, entró en la cándida colmena de su vida. (50)

. . . se le apareció, convidándole a cumplir su siniestro propósito, una especie de "hombre" de sonrisa amable y vestido de negro; pero casi al mismo tiempo, del otro lado de él surgió otra aparición, vestida de ropas cándidas, a cuya vista la primera, indudablemente un genio malo, retrocedió y se fue desvaneciendo poco a poco, hasta disiparse en absoluto. (61)

The most striking differences to be noted between *Peregrina* and the earlier novels in the use of color, besides the expanded palette noted earlier, are 1) an increased tendency to evoke subtler shades of the generic colors, 2) much more emphasis on the descriptive function, and 3) virtually no emphasis on the symbolic.

As in the earlier novels, and particularly as might be expected in a *criollista* novel, the language employed in the evocation of color is often non-metaphoric, as in "mangos color de rosa, o de púrpura, o de oro en fusión, cuando no de color de verde claro, salpicado de aquellos puntos negros" (121). However, metaphors are not uncommon, and in fact it is interesting to note in the opening chapter an image that is very reminiscent of the recurrent *rosas del crepúsculo* of *Idolos*: "Sobre el barbecho se abre aún la rosa de la tarde, cuando ya cierra la noche en el cafetal" (97). Another striking image describes the same sunset: "Gladiolas dispersas entre los rosales, erigen sus vástagos floridos, como lanzas enhiestas bajo el crepúsculo. En las puntas de algunas de esas lanzas brilla el oro y en las puntas de otras la sangre, como si fuese al golpe de ellas que el crepúsculo dorado y sangriento entró en agonía" (98).

The evocation of subtler shades of generic colors is more common than in *Sangre*, and much more so than in *Idolos*. Although, as in *Sangre*, shading is usually done with green, other colors are shaded to a greater extent than in either of the earlier novels, especially *Sangre*. The shading is usually achieved, as in the earlier novels, by the use of a modifying adjective or phrase: *verde obscuro* (108), *verde negro* (109), *blanco suavemente áureo* (110), *claras amatistas* (117), *verde intenso* (118), *un rosa tierno y traslúcido* (118), *suave glauco* (118), *morado suave, ligeramente malva* (118), *morado oscuro* (118), *verde claro* (121, 148), *casi blanco* (126), *azul negro* (126), *color de guarapo* (126), *cobrizo desmayado* (111), *flamante gradación de oro, ocres y rojo* (186), *gama infinita del verde* (186), *leve tono verdoso* (197). Occasionally the two terms are written as one word: *verdinegro* (109), *verdeobscuro* (112), *pardoamarillento* (111). As might be expected, these shadings almost always describe aspects of the natural setting, usually foliage, but occasionally other elements such as flowers, fruit, or stone.

The increased use of modifiers to suggest subtler shades of basic colors, as well as the increased use of brown, purple and silver, and the introduction of orange, is an interesting combination of *modernista* technique with the shift to a more *criollista* orientation and its emphasis on the details of the landscape. This "hybridization" is also to be noted when a wide range of colors is evoked, as this technique is used especially in the description of local *flora* as well:

Los helechos debían ser enanos, porque así los prefería la clientela, ya de un verde intenso, ya de un suave glauco de agua, ya de color de ciertas algas marinas, un rosa tierno y traslúcido. . . . pero las más queridas y buscadas . . . eran, sobre todas, las flores de mayo, de un morado suave, ligeramente malva, las unas, de un morado obscuro las . otras . . . (118)

A la flamante gradación de oro, ocres y rojos que, desde la tierra cobriza de los últimos contrafuertes del cerro, iba, pasando por todos los tonos, a vencer en la púrpura del bucare, casi de un modo súbito siguió la gama infinita del verde. El fuego, la sangre y la púrpura del verano quedaban apenas como un recuerdo glorioso en las copas de acacias y marías. En cosa de horas, privados de su flor, los bucares lucieron vestidos de hojas nuevas, y las

de aquellos en cuya flor prevalece el amarillo sobre el rojo, vueltas de revés al rudo soplo
de la brisa, despedían un vivo fulgor de plata. (186)

Colors are occasionally associated with the emotions of characters, but this tendency is greatly attenuated in comparison with the other novels. *Azul* is associated once with Amaro's happiness early in the novel: "Una sombra no más enturbiaba el azul de su alegría" (108). In a passage quite reminiscent of *Idolos*, although much briefer in extension and lacking the intense sensuality of the association as it is applied to Alberto Soria, the red color of *bucares* is associated with the all-consuming passion Bruno feels for Peregrina: "Algunos bucares, a la linde del cafetal o del barbecho, eran un solo y vasto encendimiento de púrpura. Y debajo de ellos pasó Bruno con otro incendio en el alma: un loco incendio de amor, de vanidad atormentada y herida, de inexplicable tortura de celos" (130). Red, via the association with fire, is also linked to the anger of Peregrina's father when he learns of her pregnancy: "La cólera de Feliciano fue como rancho de paja sorprendido por el fuego en pleno estío: una sola llamarada impetuosa que se alza magnífica a los cielos" (173).

Beyond these few examples there is no symbolic use of color to be noted, and it is in this stylistic shift that the evolution of Díaz Rodríguez as a colorist is most evident. The associations of color with emotions or ideas which is quite obvious in *Idolos*, and greatly expanded and refined in *Sangre*, cannot be said to be a significant element of the style of *Peregrina*, in which color is employed frequently and effectively, but with an almost completely decorative function.

Auditory Sensations

Allusions to sounds are common in all the novels, references to voices, music, and water appearing most frequently. Allusions to music are most common in *Sangre*, as might be expected. The sound of cicadas, which appears once in *Peregrina* and not all in *Sangre*, plays a prominent role in sections of *Idolos*. The total range of sounds is noticeably greater in *Peregrina*, including many sounds related to the rural setting which do not appear in the other works. There are further differences to be noted in the application of specific techniques: the use of figurative language to evoke sound, the evocation of imaginary sounds, extended emphasis on specific sounds, the use of onomatopoeia, the attribution of a symbolic function to particular sounds, and the integration of symbolic sounds into structural elements.

In *Idolos* the principal allusions are to water, music, voices (including *gritos*, crying and laughter), and cicadas. In most cases the sound evoked is a real one, that is, it is actually perceived by a character, or is meant to be perceived as real by the reader. In these allusions the language may be purely descriptive and non-metaphoric as in "el tenue susurrar de las plegarias y el timbre apagado de las voces en las naves" (336), or when "una de las muy alegres primas de Uribe . . . rasgueaba zurdamente una guitarra" (329).

18

Quite frequently the sound evoked is real, and the language employed is metaphoric, as when "las bocas de Teresa y de María desgranaron una risa alegre" (205), or "las olas . . . se rompen contra el malecón, restallando como látigos o retumbando como truenos" (325). In some cases the sound is not actually perceived but only imagined, as in the long passages in which Alberto "hears" the voice of a *sombra* awakened by his jealousy of María's former suitor, which threatens to make his life miserable if he persists in dwelling on the immutable past (300-301, 305-306). Or a real sound may suggest to the hearer another, imaginary, one: "en el melancólico rumor de queja que las gotas de agua alcanzaban al caer, antojábasele a Alberto oír un reproche" (316). Some sounds are purely figurative, as when "una alegría impetuosa entra cantando en su alma" (233), and when Alberto and Teresa are said to be "confundiendo el grito de sus corazones insaciables y el impetuoso gritar de sus pulsos con el insostenible clamor con que la tierra, torturada de sed, clamaba a los cielos" (345).

In at least one case, the sound of cicadas which forms a sort of auditory motif in Part IV, and which is often evoked through the use of language that is quite metaphoric, the sound may be said to be symbolic. The sharp, monotonous song of the insects saturates the city and the countryside in the summer:

> De cada árbol, de cada arbusto brotaba el monótono canto anunciador del estío. Cerca y lejos, cada mancha de verdura, cada rama, cada hoja, era un chirrido estridente, insostenible, como la nota más alta y gloriosa de una cuerda hecha de cristal que estuviese vibrando hasta romper de frenesí o de júbilo. . . . Y como en un grandísimo templo gótico van las columnas, los arcos y las demás partes del edificio enlazándose y fundiéndose de modo harmónico a rematar en la suprema esbeltez de la aguja, así los cantos y los coros dispersos por toda la ciudad se enlazaban y fundían en la atmósfera, sobre la ciudad ebria de bullicio y de sol, primero en un vasto coro unánime, y, por fin, en un solo grito desesperado que volaba hasta el cielo como un dardo impetuoso. (321, see also 345, 346, 358-59)

The omnipresent sound, condensed metaphorically into a single impulse, is transferred in Alberto's consciousness to a "cry" by the parched earth, and then, by means of metaphorical parallels drawn with the terms *fiebre*, *clamor* and *grito*, to an internalized "cry" in his own being:

> La tierra tenía fiebre. . . . También él, como la tierra, tenía fiebre . . . La tierra, en su fiebre, con sus árboles atormentados de sed, con sus follajes ardidos, con sus florescencias rojas, con sus innúmeros cantos de cigarras, no era sino un solo clamor que exigía del cielo inclemente la gracia de la lluvia. Así en todo él, como en la tierra febricitante, no había sino un solo deseo, una sola ansiedad, un grito solo: Teresa. (322)

Alberto realizes that although the earth's fever will be broken by the coming of rain, his own will not pass so easily and will eventually rob him of what he values most, "razón e independencia de hombre, y entusiasmo y genio de artista, para no dejar dentro de él sino lo que deja toda fiebre, lo que deja todo incendio: pavesas, ruinas, despojos" (341). At this point a clear indication of still another fever may be perceived--a revolution has broken out, and it too will leave only debris, ashes, and ruins, including those of Alberto's statues and his hopes of realizing his artistic aspirations in his own country. A short time later, as he prepares to flee from possible imprisonment because of his brother's support of the revolution, the sound of the cicadas again dominates his consciousness, and he remarks to himself, "Es la fiebre de la tierra" (359).

A similar treatment of auditory sensations is to be in noted in *Sangre*. The most frequently occurring sounds are of music, on which there is noticeably more emphasis than in *Idolos*, water, especially the sea, and voices. As in *Idolos*, sounds are usually perceived as real, and the language employed in their evocation may be purely descriptive and non-metaphoric, as in Tulio's sister-in-law's cry of grief (9), Tulio's own sobs (27, 32), or the sound of the steps of Tulio's forbear, the nun (13). However, even when the sounds are real, as they usually are, they occur much more frequently in metaphors than is the case in *Idolos*. This is particularly true in the allusions to music, where flowers are often an element of the image. Martí's music is likened to "flores frágiles, trabajadas con la substancia inmaterial del sonido" (48), or to a "sonora lluvia de pétalos impalpables" (48), or to "melodiosas flores frágiles" (50). The first notes of Schumann's *Träumerei*, played by the enigmatic Sra. Perales on board Tulio's homeward bound ship, are compared to "resonantes pétalos cristalinos" (82).

Imaginary sounds occur in *Sangre* as well. The most obvious example occurs in chapter II when Tulio's incipient neurosis causes him to imagine that his failure to adopt a direction for his life has angered his ancestors. In a manner reminiscent of Alberto Soria's *sombra*, they seem to speak to him; in this case it is through his ancestral home:

> La sorda hostilidad se propagaba por las paredes, entrando en las habitaciones, meciendo
> los pilares, invadiéndolo todo, hasta colmar la casa con un solo vórtice de ira. A cada
> paso, bajo sus pies nacían miles de voces, no de reproche ni de ruego, sino de amenaza,
> que iban tras él, acompañándole, persiguiéndole, como un coro implacable de furias. (17)

A similar example occurs in chapter IV, where the Paris apartment Tulio has so lovingly prepared for Belén also has a "voice:" "Pero los objetos y las almas de los objetos, burlados en su espera, en vez de romper en un concierto epitalámico, prorrumpieron, desgarrada su harmonía, en la música disonante del sollozo" (30).

As in *Idolos*, sounds may be purely figurative. Martí's early attraction to music is compared to a "débil e inesperado repicar de notas cristalinas" (47), and he learns of various religious sects, which are "corriendo y cantando como fuentes claras bajo la atmósfera turbia de mercantilismo" (50). The sea is often personified through the use of *cantar* or *reír*. This is especially true in the final chapter, in which a *leitmotif* of which the laughter of the sea is an element occurs several times: "El mar, hasta perderse de vista, reía y retozaba con un continuo cabrilleo" (77, see also 81, 87, 90, 92, 94). It may also be said that this figurative sound has some symbolic force since, as various critics have pointed out, the sea itself is symbolic (Benítez 263, Castro 61, Debicki 64-65, Fraser 11-12, Olivares, "Disposición, argumento . . ." 23, Persaud 199-203). The persistent figurative laughter suggests indifference to human suffering, and emphasizes the function of the sea as the seductive and malevolent force that Fraser (11) and Olivares ("Disposición, argumento . . ." 23) have perceived.

The metaphoric intermingling of the suggestive symbolism of aquatic elements with auditory sensations is most apparent in a passage which has been singled out by some critics as a prime example of Díaz Rodríguez' stylistic virtuosity (Olivares, "Disposición, argumento . . ." 27, Phillips 285, Unamuno 375). It is the extended paragraph in which the musical composition intended to illustrate Martí's exposition of the basic laws of music is described. Here it will be noted that auditory sensations are evoked not only through words the meaning of which suggests certain sounds, but also through onomatopoeia, a device that is not to be noted to any significant extent in *Idolos* or *Peregrina*:

> Primero fue arriba en el teclado, una nota muy tenue, como la que produce el caer de una débil gota de agua sobre un cristal sonoro; tras de ella vino otra, y otra, y otra nota semejante que llegaron, multiplicándose y cada vez menos tenues, a fingir el caer precipitado de una lluvia muy fina; al repiqueteo de la lluvia muy fina siguió el deslizarse tembloroso de un hilo de agua entre las altas hierbas; luego se oyeron las quejumbres, las canciones y las risas de la acequia rebosante; en seguida resonó el tumultuario estrépito del torrente y este mismo estrépito, serenándose poco a poco, se cambió en el rumor sereno y apacible del río, rumor que, a medida se hinchaba el río fue haciéndose más grave y reposado, hasta desaparecer más lejos, en donde los grandes ríos, entre sus márgenes remotas, corren y se extienden con majestad oceánica, en medio del silencio más augusto. (65)

The passage continues, describing a brief interlude of melody, and then reversing the order of the aquatic elements to return to the single drop of rain.

The rain and the tumultuous river are described as being more active than the other phenomena, and must therefore be imagined to be more boisterous. In the nouns used to refer to these phenomena, *repiqueteo* and *estrépito*, most of the consonants are voiceless stops, [p], [t], and [k], which create a harsher effect on the ear than do most other Spanish consonants. On the other hand, in the words used to refer to the slower moving streams, *deslizarse, tembloroso, rumor,* and *sereno*, most of the consonants are continuants, [s], [l], [m], and [n], which are less "noisy" to the ear, and in addition create a certain impression of flowing motion as opposed to the choppy movement suggested by the phonetic stops. [5]

This passage, in addition to illustrating stylistic techniques, is of course closely tied to the structure of the novel, since the suggestive power of water (and of the color green) is instrumental in inducing the dream state which culminates in Tulio's suicide.

Auditory sensations abound in *Peregrina*. As in *Idolos* and *Sangre* there are evocations of music, sounds of water, and voices, but these sounds, none of which really predominates in the novel, are augmented by a large number of others which do not occur in the other novels. Not surprisingly, most of them are sounds made by animals--chickens (97), cattle (101), dogs (103, 105, 144, 147, 148), bulls (106), birds (104, 108, 116, 148), and insects (105, 108, 123, 169, 172, 186)--or sounds that have strong associations with rural life--wind (101, 133, 182), wind in trees (101, 182), or in bamboo (114), thunder (182, 185), rain (187), carts (113), or the sound of coffee beans falling to the ground (131).

The manner in which sounds are evoked is quite similar to that employed in *Idolos* and *Sangre*. Almost all the sounds are perceived as real, and the language employed is quite frequently non-metaphoric, as when "las muchachas disimulan su desazón lanzando risitas ahogadas" (102), or when two bulls "contestándose mugido a mugido . . . llenaban todo el valle con su clamorosa quejumbre" (106). In the evocation of a large number of auditory sensations, however, the language is metaphoric, as in the description of the sound issuing from the schoolhouse: "dentro de un decrépito caserón, como ilusión juvenil en un alma de viejo, se hospedaba el sordo y monótono rumor del colmenar de la escuela del pueblo" (121), or when laughter is compared to the sound of birds: "una risa loca estalló entre las peñas, como un pájaro burlón que estallara de alegría" (164). A number of images are considerably more modernistic than the foregoing, as when "una risa fresca y sonora desgrana en la sombra del cafetal su cantarín chorro de perlas" (99), or when "un chaguaramo, sobre su armonioso fuste de columna coríntica, despliega sonoramente su abanico de palmas" (101).

In two passages there is to be noted a tendency to focus at some length on a single auditory sensation, a technique similar to that employed in *Idolos* in the evocation of the sound of the cicadas and in *Sangre* in the passage describing Martí's composition. However, the extended evocations in *Peregrina* are in no way

22

related to the structure of the novel, as they are in *Idolos* and *Sangre*, but rather serve to emphasize the rural setting. One of these passages concentrates on the sound of birds:

El matapalo era asilo, comedero y alcoba nupcial de todos los pájaros del bosque. Apenas el cucarachero, gris como el ruiseñor y matinal como la alondra, indomesticable por bravío aunque de hábitos domésticos porque suele acogerse a las viviendas humanas, cantaba sobre los muros de la huerta, en el tejado del repartimiento y en los alrededores de la casa grande, ya estaba el matapalo vibrando todo de cantos, aleteos y trinos como una poblada y gigantesca pajarera. De los primeros en aparecer . . . los gonzalitos, con sus plumas de un negro luciente y de un vivo anaranjado, rasgaban como relámpagos el verde claro de las hojas. Y como dóciles a un rito, al nacer el sol, rompían todos juntos en concertada y melodiosa orquesta de flautas. . . . A manera de gavilán, el cristofué se posaba en la propia cima del árbol a dar desde ahí de cuando en cuando, el grito monótono y único de donde el nombre le viene. . . . Y entre los más numerosos, aunque no de los más pequeños, los azulejos, trajeados de azul, se ganaban por su algarabía las palmas del escándalo. Pendencieros, en continuo debate por la comida y el amor, escandalizaban con sus revuelos y chillidos. (148-49)

What is immediately apparent here is the emphasis on the variety of birds and on the detail of the sounds made by them, an emphasis entirely in keeping with the *criollista* focus of the novel. The same emphasis on variety and detail is to be noted in a passage describing the sound of crickets, in which it will also be noted that the imagery is quite modernistic:

Dentro y fuera del repartimiento, bajo la arboleda del cafetal, resuena y se prolonga la orquesta de los grillos. En ella el oído avezado reconoce muchas variedades de estilos e instrumentos. Hay maestros menudos que sacan una fina nota de vidrio de su violincito estridente; los hay que tienen una nota aflautada y sedeña de viola, y otros grandes, como grandes tazas grises, cuyas notas parecen notas de violoncelo, profundas. (105)

The personification in both passages, especially in the second, lends a light-hearted note, bordering on humor in the case of the cricket musicians, which is not to be found in any evocations of auditory sensations, or anywhere else for that matter, in *Idolos* or *Sangre*.

The characters in *Peregrina* do not hear imaginary voices. The young girls, however, do hear on occasion a strange music issuing from the *pozo encantado* as they fill their water jugs or do their laundry. The music seems to be connected to some atavistic compulsion which may lead them, as it does Peregrina, first to love and then to death. The final lines of the novel summarize this connection:

23

Las mozas de los contornos oirán de nuevo resonar en el seno del agua la misma vieja y suave música de arpas y violines. Bastará que una de ellas, flor de belleza rústica, se mire en el trémulo cristal del pozo, conturbada por la música y el recóndito misterio de ciertas palabras. Bastará que alrededor de una de ellas, flor de belleza rústica, empiecen a tejer su ronda, eterna y mágica, los dos hermanos gemelos e invencibles: el Amor y la Muerte. (198)

This sound belongs, rather than to the realm of psychology, as do the voices heard by Alberto Soria and Tulio Arcos, to that of folk myth and superstition.[6]

There are some purely figurative sounds in *Peregrina*, which are often based on terms related to music or laughter. Amaro's secret love for Peregrina "amenazaba sofocarlo, . . . resonando dentro de él a manera de una música" (176). In two figurative evocations of sound reminiscent of the laughing sea motif of *Sangre*, although without the structured repetition, nature is personified as laughing, indifferent to the suffering of Peregrina and of man in general:

Rieron los peones; rieron las cogedoras de café; y la misma naturaleza, en aquel instante, pareció tomar parte en la risa, multiplicando al infinito la burla. Seres y cosas de lo hondo del valle surgían como desternillándose de risa en el ambiente diáfano y risueño. . . . Y mientras musiú Pedro, maliciando desde un principio la burla, se mesaba los cabellos y bramaba letanías de maldiciones debajo de su cobertizo de zinc, . . . Peregrina miraba ya correr, descubierto y divulgado, por veredas y caminos, con el secreto de los fantasmas, el secreto de su vergüenza y de su amor. (153-54)

Entretanto, indiferente a la dicha y a la miseria de los hombres, en una atmósfera quieta y clarísima como una gema diáfana, el Avila se erguía sereno y sin nube. Entretanto, sobre la burla y el dolor, la naturaleza, indiferente, reía. En la plena algidez veraniega, de este a oeste, de norte a sur, estallaba la risa de la naturaleza en la rojez clamorosa de los bucares. (158)

Although the imaginary music that issues periodically from the *pozo encantado* may be viewed as being marginally "symbolic," through its link to folk myth and superstition, its connection with the plot is tenuous at best. Like the other references to superstitions in the novel (for example, ghosts and buried treasures), it must be considered to be primarily descriptive of the way of life of the *campesinos*.

Olfactory Sensations

Evocations of olfactory sensations are less common in all the novels than color and auditory sensations, but they occur frequently enough to be considered to be a significant stylistic device. The range of terms used to evoke olfactory sensations is very similar in all the novels; forms of *perfume* and *fragancia* are the most common, other terms occurring occasionally (see Table III). Flowers may also suggest fragrance; however, flower names *per se* are not used for this purpose as, for example, *rosa* or *lila* may by itself suggest a color. As in the case of evocations of color, the total frequency of all olfactory words is highest in *Sangre*. It is lowest in *Peregrina*, which may be somewhat unexpected, but this decreased emphasis suggests that Díaz Rodríguez associated olfactory sensations more with the modernistic orientation than with his brand of *criollismo*. Differences in specific usage are to be noted in the relative prevalence of actual and figurative odors, and pleasant and unpleasant odors, and in specific associations of odors with other elements.

In *Idolos* actual odors are usually of flowers, of women's flesh or hair, and of perfume (notably that used by Teresa Farías). In fact, actual odors are more often associated with Teresa than in any other single context. She bathes in a mixture of milk and perfume (337, 338, 342), and the excessive piety that counterbalances her intense sexuality is associated with the odor of incense in cathedrals (334, 338). Olfactory sensations play a significant role in the description of the bedroom adjoining Alberto's studio, which serves as the meeting place for their illicit affair. In the most detailed description of this room, perceived through María's jealous senses, the emphasis on flowers and perfume is extended to include the essence of the act of love itself, a touch of realism and intensity of a type that will not recur in the other novels:

> Si en la estatua no adivinó [María] el símbolo de la voluptuosidad, sí percibió su perfume
> en el ambiente de la alcoba. Es perfume que no engaña. No engaña ni a la prostituta, ni a
> la virgen, tal vez menos a la virgen que a la prostituta. Quien jamás lo conoció, lo *reconoce*
> al percibirlo. Ese perfume, olor de carne y esencia de besos y caricias, mezclado ahí a
> fragancia de flores y al perfume que María conoció por ser el perfume preferido de Teresa,
> llenaba la alcoba y parecía exhalarse del lecho y sus ropas y cortinajes finísimos, de las
> paredes, del tocador, y de todos los demás muebles de aquel rincón de taller convertido,
> por obra y gracia de la voluptuosidad, en *boudoir* elegante y deleitoso. (365)

Figurative evocations of odors are more frequent than non-figurative, although not greatly so. These are often linked to the notion of love as well, as when Alberto, realizing he is in love with María, feels that "de todas partes venían a él, acariciando sus manos, acariciando su frente, un vaho de frescura y una ola de fragancias" (246). Teresa's hands, with which he becomes obsessed, "esparcían fragancia como flores" (340). Odors are also linked figuratively to the notion of beauty in descriptions of one of Alberto's statues: "la escultura destinada a perpetuar un peregrino fulgor de belleza, la estatua de la mulatica del Tuy fresca y primorosa, como hecha de barro blondo, fragancia de canela y zumo de flores de apamate" (376, see also 220 and 267). In another passage figurative odors are linked to the notion of the redemption of the republic. As the visionary Emazábel explains the task to his compatriots, "en el alma de éste y en las palabras con que él decía la magnitud o delineaba los grandes lineamentos de la obra, la obra aparecía derramando, como perfume de vida, como hálitos de selvas primaverales, tesoros de una belleza nueva, belleza militante, belleza heroica: la belleza de la acción" (287, see also 293 and 295).

Although actual odors in *Idolos* are almost always pleasant (there is an allusion to "acres olores de medicinas," 313) the figurative odors are sometimes unpleasant. The *sombra* that materializes out of Alberto's obsessive jealousy of María's past, warns him that if he persists in this attitude, "en vez de margaritas hallarás asfodelos, un gran campo de asfodelos, de cuyas flores irá a ti, como un perfume, a turbar tu razón, a emponzoñar tu vida, a corroer tus entrañas, la más mortal de las tristezas. . . . me sentirás en la malsana esencia de las flores" (301). Appropriately to the critical content of the work, politicians are said to treat politics "como a una gran señora, aunque ya de muy lejos la tal señora oliese a barragana. ¡Ay, de quien dijese que su olor no era olor de virtud!" (350). This odor, if not exactly unpleasant, is clearly negative in its intent.

In *Sangre* there is an increased overall use of olfactory sensations, and the balance between non-figurative and figurative odors leans very heavily toward the latter. There is, furthermore, less variety in the actual odors evoked, and more in the figurative, and an almost complete lack of unpleasant odors.

Actual odors are usually of flowers, but also include "aroma . . . de la tierra andaluza" (13), the "ráfaga de música y olores" of a spring night (72), and the only unpleasant odor, suggested rather obliquely: a reference to the ship bearing Tulio back to Venezuela, which is a "laberinto . . . nada cómodo ni bien oliente" (77-78).

Odors are associated figuratively with idyllic love, as in Tulio's "idilio, desarrollado luego por la línea verde y azul de la costa, como una doble harmonía de música y fragancia" (74, see also 4 and 27), with his family and its heroism ("la sangre les daba color, el heroísmo fragancia," 9), the ancestral home, in which "cada ángulo, cada muro, cada fresco pasadizo tenía viva sangre de historia, hechizo azul de fábula o pálida fragancia de anécdota" (16), with "el alma de las generaciones conservada como un perfume en el sutil encanto de las cosas viejas" (16), and with the voice of Tulio's great aunt, which "venía de lo más hondo de la abuela, y de toda ella se exhalaba como un perfume" (18). Fragrance is also associated with Martí, his religion, and his music: ". . . el cristianismo suyo estaba hecho de medula blanca de Evangelio,

. . . lo embalsamaba además, como aroma de floresta virgen, el misterio fragante de una vaga secta obscura" (46, see also 47 and 50). Tulio's life is once compared to a "gota de esencia" (80), and the atmosphere of Sevilla is perceived by Tulio's artist forbear to be "cargada de olor de fábula y de azahar" (54). One of the most modernistic images in the novel refers to the flowers Tulio had intended as a welcome for Belén, which are "una tremenda ironía, como debe de ser la ironía de un dios, muda y perfumada" (32), and when he decides to cast flowers on the sea, which is now her tomb, "fue como si de pronto se colmase de suavidad y tibieza, como si dentro de él, perfumándolo, se fundiesen, al calor de la sangre, muchas lágrimas de mirra" (71-72).

Olfactory sensations occur in *Peregrina* with noticeably less frequency than in *Idolos* and *Sangre*, and the range of references is significantly reduced, especially in comparison to *Sangre*.

Actual odors, which are much more common than figurative associations, are almost always of plant life: "hierba fragante" (107), the "aroma tenaz, grave y dulzón" of *nardos* (107), "la región de los inciensos, la pesgua y otras plantas de aroma" (116), "olor de jazmín" (118), "pelicanos, cuya fragancia . . . es . . . más intensa en la noche" (118), "perfume de un árbol" (150), and the "nieve fragante" of jasmines (197). It may probably be assumed that plant life contributes significantly to the fragrance of a "noche de mayo tibia y perfumada" (156). The "acre perfume" of rain is alluded to once (182), and Amaro remembers the "buen olor" of his mother's house (109).

Figurative odors, which are not frequent, are invariably associated with some aspect of love. In Peregrina's body "despertaba la voluptuosidad como un perfume" (155), and at the end of the novel the fickle Bruno, returning to the scene of the tragedy, imagines himself to be the "héroe de aquella tragedia de amor clara y fragante" (193). Amaro's unrequited love for Peregrina is twice referred to with images in which fragrance and music are combined: he loves Peregrina "en el más fragante y musical secreto de su corazón" (175), and this secret in his heart is said to be "ya resonando dentro de él a manera de una música, ya enflorándose y perfumando como un jardín en primavera" (176). Somewhat surprisingly, unpleasant odors are not found, but this must probably be attributed to the general tendency of Díaz Rodríguez to idealize in *Peregrina*, in spite of its down-to-earth *criollista* orientation.

Tactile Sensations

Terms associated with tactile sensations occur in all the novels. Forms of *beso, caricia, and suave* are used most frequently; forms of *áspero* occur less frequently, and forms of *seda* or other fabrics (*raso, terciopelo*) appear occasionally. These terms may evoke an actual tactile sensation, or be used with an alternate or figurative meaning (see Tables IV a and IV b). It comes as no surprise to note that the frequency of actual tactile sensations, especially *besos* and *caricias*, is highest in *Idolos*, with its realistic emphasis on Alberto's illicit affair with Teresa, and that the non-actual use of tactile terms is greatest in *Sangre*. Further differences are to be noted in the relative frequency of figurative language used in connection with the terms, and in the extended emphasis on specific sensations.

As in the case of the other sense impressions, actual tactile sensations may be evoked with non-metaphoric language, as in the "suavidad sedosa" which describes Teresa's skin (*Idolos* 337), the "húmedos besos y caricias" of Tulio's siren (*Sangre* 91), or the "lenguas ásperas" of bulls in *Peregrina* (134). However, in *Idolos*, and to a much greater extent in *Sangre*, evocations of actual tactile sensations frequently employ figurative language, although this is rarely the case in *Peregrina*. Teresa's hands are "suaves, como cándidos lirios de seda" (*Idolos* 340), and Tulio, preparing the Paris apartment for Belén, "sobre las cosas deshojaba la caricia," (*Sangre* 30). One of the few examples of this usage in *Peregrina* is when Bruno, contemplating the beauties of his mysterious seductress, thinks, "Aquella seda de los pechos, aquel raso de su vientre, aquel terciopelo de sus muslos, no son de una caminera" (165). The relative frequency of figurative language in the evocation of actual tactile sensations in the three novels is striking, progressing from roughly half the total number of occurrences of the terms in *Idolos* to a distribution roughly equal with that of non-figurative language in *Sangre*, and diminishing greatly in *Peregrina*.

With the exception of *terciopelo*, all the terms, especially forms of *suave*, are also used in contexts in which actual tactile sensations are not suggested. These cases may involve an alternate meaning of *suave* or *áspero*, as in the "azul muy suave" of flowers (*Idolos* 255), Martí's "áspera faena por la conquista del pan" (*Sangre* 45), or the "suave luz de la luna" in *Peregrina* (105). More frequently, however, in *Idolos* and *Sangre*, but rarely in *Peregrina*, when actual sensations are not evoked the words are used figuratively, as in "goces dulces y ásperos de la vida" (*Idolos* 251), or the "suavidades de rosa" with which Tulio's great aunt rejects her lover (*Sangre* 18). A rare example in *Peregrina* is the reference to the talent of Juan Francisco, who "posee a la perfección el arte noble de amansar, hasta hacer dóciles como una seda con alma, a los más recios y voluntariosos novillos" (97).

An equally striking difference in the use of tactile sensations in the three works is that in both *Idolos* and *Sangre* certain tactile perceptions are dwelt on at some length, whereas this is much less the case in *Peregrina*. Especially in *Idolos*, and in passages referring to Teresa Farías, either as she is perceived by Alberto or as she herself experiences certain sensations, is this to be noted. Alberto is especially fascinated by her hands: "De ellas no podía decirse que tocaban: acariciaban. En dondequiera posaran su inquietud, ya en los vestidos o en las formas de Teresa, ya en el libro de oraciones, o en otro objeto, ya en las manos o el cuello del amante, cada contacto suyo era una caricia" (340). Teresa revels in the sensations of wind and water on her body, especially the latter. As she bathes in the sea, she reacts in an intensely sensual manner:

Sintiendo por todas partes los besos de la onda, se hacía la ilusión de hallarse en poder de un amante ardiente y habilísimo, a cuyos labios expertos e insaciables no se podía esquivar la más recóndita partícula de su cuerpo desnudo. Largo tiempo se recreaba en esa ilusión del amante que de pies a cabeza la envolvía de continuo en un solo beso, mientras ella no lograba retenerlo ni un segundo entre sus brazos. (332)

A more forceful, although less straightforward, use of the device is found in the long passages describing in more detail the nature of Teresa's sensuality and its effect on Alberto. Both are described in terms of the state of their "nerves," which is influenced by various sense impressions. In these passages the sensations are not tactile in the strictest sense, but they are clearly perceived physically as well as emotionally. Teresa responds to the *chiaroscuro* effects of light and color, the sound of whispered prayers, and the odor of incense in cathedrals, which have the power to provoke intensely erotic reactions in her: "Tales sensaciones ambiguas, al condensarse y acumularse en los nervios, comunicaban a éstos una sorprendente virtud o fuerza oculta, capaz de romper al roce más débil, según los casos, en puros desmayos místicos o en voluptuosidades locas" (336). Alberto, in a state of intensely heightened sensitivity occasioned by the relationship, responds to various stimuli, however vague or tenuous: "A estímulos débiles, respondían sus nervios con resonancia maravillosa" (339). Teresa's hands are capable of inducing a range of responses in him: "Y si un solo ademán de esas manos bastaba a sacudir a Alberto con el espasmo del placer más agudo, su contacto o caricia llegaba a veces, extremando la violencia de la sensación, a cambiar de placer en espasmo doloroso" (340).

At the beginning of their affair several pages are devoted to the habit they develop of kissing one another on the sly, while they are with or near other people, but for various reasons unnoticed by them. In these passages it is not only the actual sensation of the kisses themselves that is evoked but also the physical thrill produced in the two lovers by the furtiveness of the act: "siendo tanto mayor el deleite que saboreaban en el beso, cuantos mayores riesgos corrían de ser vistos de los otros. Sobre todo en Alberto, el deleite de los besos fugaces, como súbito roce de alas, era indecible" (330).

In *Sangre* the sensation of water on flesh associated with the beginning of Tulio's recurrent dream is emphasized: "quedaba envolviendo a Tulio por todas partes un cosquilleo delicioso, como la múltiple caricia de un agua efervescente" (36, see also 37 and 67). But the sensuality of *Idolos* is lacking. Although the sensation experienced by Tulio is compared to a caress, and, because the dream revolves around a reunion with his dead wife, indirectly suggests a physical relationship, this relationship is in fact quite chaste and does not progress physically beyond kissing. There is, moreover, no emphasis on the tactile sensation of kisses; rather they are said to be the "flor del idilio," and are associated with the salt taste of the sea (76).

Similar instances of emphasis on tactile sensations are lacking in *Peregrina*. Although water also figures prominently at the end of that novel, there are no tactile sensations associated with it. Nor are there any significant erotic overtones associated with tactile sensations in the novel. While we know that the physical relationship between Peregrina and Bruno is quite as intense and passionate as that between Teresa and Alberto (unlike the idealized relationship between Belén and Tulio), there is relatively little emphasis either on the sensuality of Peregrina herself or the effect of her physical charms on Bruno, another example of the author's distancing himself from reality.

Sensations of Taste

In all the novels Díaz Rodríguez uses words related to taste sensations, but less frequently than is the case with any of the other sense related words do these evoke actual sensations. In most cases the terms are used with an alternate or figurative meaning (see Tables V a and V b).

Words suggesting sweetness are the most common in all the works, occurring most frequently in *Sangre* and *Peregrina*. Not surprisingly, in view of its negative tone, words suggesting bitterness are fairly common in *Idolos*, occurring with about half the frequency of those suggesting sweetness, whereas these terms are rare in the other two works. Occurring occasionally in all the works are words suggesting acid or sour taste. A salt taste (of the sea, of course) is evoked only in *Sangre*. Forms of *sabor* appear quite frequently in all the works. There are further differences between the novels in the use of figurative language in connection with the terms, and it is interesting to note that although Díaz Rodríguez de-emphasizes olfactory sensations in the *criollista Peregrina*, the incidence of actual taste sensations is highest here (although not significantly, in comparison to *Sangre*), and *Peregrina* is, furthermore, the only novel to mention specific food flavors.[7] There are no actual taste sensations evoked in *Idolos*.

With the exception of a figurative association of *dulce* and *fruto* in *Sangre* (12), and the linking of *dulce* and *caña* in *Peregrina* (114 and 123), in none of the novels do forms of *dulce* refer to an actual sweet taste. Rather they are used in the sense of "gentle," "soft," "pleasant," or "agreeable," as in "el dulce regalo de una jira artística por la Italia del Norte" (*Idolos* 268), "las dulzuras del poder" (*Idolos* 277), "melancolía dulce" (*Idolos* 311), "las dulzuras del pecado" (*Idolos* 331), "lágrimas dulces" (*Sangre* 25), "sueño dulce" (*Sangre* 36), "dulce embriaguez de los narcóticos" (*Sangre* 69), "la timidez muy dulce de los idilios castos" (*Sangre* 74), "dulce noche lívida" (*Peregrina* 105), "palabras dulces" (*Peregrina* 153), "dulce belleza de oro, de ámbar y miel de Peregrina" (*Peregrina* 173), and "dulzuras del pastoreo" (*Peregrina* 174).

30

Forms of *amargo* almost never evoke actual sensations of taste. In *Idolos* and *Sangre*, especially *Idolos*, they usually refer to another kind of bitterness, which may be evoked figuratively: "el aplauso mejor . . . no llegó al alma de Soria, sino destilando amargura" (*Idolos* 188), "la anticipada amargura de un remordimiento" (*Idolos* 190), "la amargura del desengaño" (*Sangre* 38). The sharp, bitter taste of the sea is evoked in both novels, but in *Idolos* the sensation is an element of an image that does not evoke an actual taste: "Y las preguntas . . . retrocedían de los labios, dejando en éstos un poco de su corrosiva acerbidad, como en las playas deja la onda algo de su amargura indestructible" (303). In *Sangre* the bitterness of sea water is alluded to in an image: "el corazón del océano, amargo y profundo" (68), and only once is an actual taste sensation perceived, or at least imagined, by Tulio. Speaking of the nightly visits of his imaginary mermaid, he tells Borja, "Sus labios dejan en los míos la amargura del océano" (91). In *Peregrina*, in which *amargo* appears only once, it refers to the actual taste of beer, which is "amarga y negra" (145).

Acerbo and *acerbidad* are always used in senses that do not evoke actual taste sensations, and which may be figurative; this is usually the case with *ácido* as well, as in the example above from *Idolos* (303), or in "acerba nostalgia" (*Idolos* 291), or a reference to Tulio's great aunt's voice, which is compared to "un ácido celeste" (*Sangre* 18), or to a comment by one of the minor characters in *Peregrina*, which is made with "siniestra acerbidad" (170). *Acido* describes the actual taste of blackberries in *Peregrina*; the fruit of certain bushes is said to be "áspero y ácido, aunque no tan áspero y ácido como el que se cría entre los zarzales del cerro" (122).

Aspero and *aspereza* do not usually refer to tastes, but rather to tactile sensations. In *Idolos áspero* is contrasted once with *dulce*, and therefore does belong in the realm of taste, but an actual taste is not evoked; Alberto's brother tells him that he wants to savor life to the fullest, with all its "goces dulces y ásperos" (251). Only in *Peregrina*, where blackberries are said to be "fruto . . . sabrosísimo y áspero" (116), and in the example cited above (122) is an actual sour taste evoked.

A salt taste is evoked only in *Sangre*. On waking from his dream, Tulio tastes, or imagines, on his lips "la salsedumbre de la ola" (39, 76).

Sabor, *saborear* and *sabroso* rarely refer to actual taste sensations. Food flavors are alluded to rather vaguely in *Sangre*, once in a general sense, when the ship passengers anticipate savoring a meal on shore (24), and once figuratively to describe Borja, who is "de aquella especie de hombres que se aprenden a querer, como se aprende a saborear ciertos manjares, de sabor disimulado y ambiguo" (40). In the description of blackberries cited above (*Peregrina* 116), of course, *sabrosísimo* does refer to their actual taste, and in another example of the rare actual taste sensations in *Peregrina* the opossum is said to have "aristocráticos gustos, por su irresistible tendencia a alimentarse de naranjas y de sabrosa carne de gallina"

31

(144). However, especially in *Idolos*, in which the occurrence of the terms is considerably higher than in the later works, either an alternate meaning or a figurative use is usually involved. Alberto savors the sunsets in Macuto (*Idolos* 324, 325), and the Blanco family of *Peregrina* can predictably be found at a certain time each Sunday "saboreando las primeras dulzuras de su champurrio" (166). *Sabroso* is used in the densely figurative description of Martí's life in *Sangre*: "La trabajaba como una azucena, con la seda cándida y firme de su virtud; a la imagen y semejanza de una azucena en cuyo fondo se hubiese alojado, a fabricar panales de miel sabrosa, un enjambre de melodías" (49).

As is the case in the use of other sense related terms, the proportion of figurative language occurring in references to taste is significantly higher in *Sangre*; it is quite low in both *Idolos* and *Peregrina*.

As has been seen, the evocation of sense impressions, one of the most striking features of Díaz Rodríguez' style, is prevalent in all of the novels. By far the most common of these are allusions to color; the evocation of sounds is next in frequency, and odors, tactile sensations, and taste are evoked less frequently. The total concentration of all sense impressions is highest in *Sangre* and lowest in *Idolos,* but while the concentration of color, olfactory, tactile, and taste impressions is significantly higher in *Sangre* than in the other two novels, evocations of sound are most frequent, and most varied, in *Peregrina*.

Red is the predominant color in all the novels except *Sangre*, in which green occurs somewhat more frequently. The other frequently occurring colors--green, blue, white, and yellow--are given varied degrees of emphasis. Although the density of color is greater in *Sangre* the range of colors in it is the most limited of the three works. Not appearing at all in *Sangre* are some colors which do appear, although rarely, in *Idolos* and with somewhat more frequency in *Peregrina*--purple, brown, and silver. The palette of *Peregrina* may be said to be the widest of the three works, not only because it includes orange (albeit only once), which is not found in either of the other novels, but because the range of terms employed to evoke some colors is also wider. Shading of generic colors, evocations of a gamut of color, and the use of metaphoric language increase from *Idolos* to *Sangre*. In *Peregrina* shading increases somewhat more, and evocations of a wide range of color occur with about equal frequency as in *Sangre*. The use of figurative language in the evocation of color is not as evident in *Peregrina* as in the earlier novels, especially *Sangre*, but it does occur. Color sometimes has a symbolic function in *Idolos*, and the use of this device is greatly increased in *Sangre*. In *Peregrina* the function of color, which is very frequently linked to natural phenomena, is virtually completely decorative.

There is a greater variety of sounds in *Peregrina* than in either of the earlier novels, and a marked tendency to associate auditory sensations with natural phenomena. In the evocation of auditory sensations there is a predilection for metaphor in *Sangre* that is less evident in the other two novels, although these do not lack figurative sounds. In *Idolos* and *Sangre* auditory sensations are sometimes linked to the structure of the works, which is not the case in *Peregrina*, and in the two earlier novels the protagonists hear imaginary voices as a symptom of their psychological states, whereas in *Peregrina* the only imaginary sound that occurs is the music that originates in the *pozo encantado*, and this is a ramification of folk belief rather than of psychological pathology.

Olfactory sensations occur more frequently in *Sangre* than in the other novels, and they are more often figurative. Only in *Idolos* is there any real emphasis on unpleasant odors, and in *Idolos* an element of sensuality is sometimes associated with olfactory sensations. In *Peregrina* odors, which are usually not figurative, are very frequently associated with nature.

Words associated with tactile sensations often do not evoke actual sensations. In *Idolos,* and to a greater extent in *Sangre*, these cases often involve figurative language. Figurative language is seldom used in *Peregrina*. The tendency to dwell on certain tactile sensations at some length is much more marked in *Idolos* and *Sangre* than in *Peregrina*, and in *Idolos* these sensations, like some odors, are sometimes associated with an element of sensuality.

Taste associated words very seldom suggest actual taste sensations. There are no actual tastes evoked in *Idolos,* and very few in *Sangre*, and these are quite indirect. Only in *Peregrina* do a few genuine references to taste occur. The proportion of figurative language used is again highest in *Sangre* and lowest in *Peregrina*. Forms of *dulce* far outnumber all other taste associated words in all the novels, but in *Idolos* words suggesting non-actual bitterness are much more common than in *Sangre,* and they do not occur in *Peregrina*.

NOTES

[1] The original title of *Sangre* was *Uvas del trópico*. The title *Sangre patricia,* of course, is more appropriate to the plot, with its emphasis on the protagonist's lineage, but it also forms an effective link with the color suggestive use of *sangre* in the novel.

[2] For a discussion of this function of color see Matteson "The Symbolic Use of Color in Díaz Rodríguez' *Sangre patricia*."

[3] Red imagery, referring to mortification of the flesh, is linked to the notion of heroism, but serves here to clarify the mystic nature of the nun's existence.

4 See Matteson, "The Symbolic Use of Color in Díaz Rodríguez' *Sangre patricia*," (39).

5 See Persaud (199-200) for other examples of onomatopoeia in *Sangre patricia*.

6 Torres Rioseco interprets it is an example of "ese sentimiento de misterio que se apodera de nuestro ánimo en presencia de lo desconocido; el temblor del alma en los umbrales de la metafísica" (86).

7 Latcham, referring to Díaz Rodríguez' talent for evoking sense impressions, notes that "llama la atención en sus libros la absoluta carencia de descripciones de manjares, de comidas, de sutilezas gastronómicas" (26). This assertion can hardly be contested. It is interesting to note, however, that in the novels only *Peregrina*, with its *criollista* focus, has any specific mention of food flavors at all.

CHAPTER II

"FAVORITE" WORDS

The reader of Díaz Rodríguez' three novels cannot fail to notice the repeated use of certain nouns and adjectives, which appear to have some special appeal for the author. Among the most common of these are *alma, belleza* or *bello, diáfano* (*diafanidad* once), *idílico* or *idilio, ensueño* or *sueño*, and *voluptuosidad* or *voluptuoso*. (see Table VI).

Alma

His fascination with the noun *alma*, the most frequently occurring of the "favorite words," is most evident in *Idolos*; it decreases somewhat in *Sangre*, and there is a marked decrease in its use in *Peregrina*. In all the novels *alma* usually connotes the related ideas of "soul," "mind," "spirit," or "being," and refers to these aspects of human beings.

Alberto Soria's first glimpses of the streets of Caracas after his return from Paris produce a "dolor abierto de súbito en su alma como la rosa de una herida" (*Idolos* 198), Belén's fellow passengers, on arriving in France, "abrigaban la cruel esperanza de ver cómo saltaría, en los ojos y el alma de un hombre, un gran dolor improviso y desnudo" (*Sangre* 24-25), and the fiery color of *bucares* parallels the emotions of Bruno, who has "otro incendio en el alma: un loco incendio de amor" (*Peregrina* 130). Occasionally the connotation is extended to groups of human beings. The intellectual minority to which Alberto, Emazábel and their fellow reformers belong is a "núcleo de almas selectas" (*Idolos* 230), Tulio berates himself for having lowered his ideal, "hasta hacerlo accesible a toda alma plebeya" (*Sangre* 34), and in *Peregrina* the legend of spirits flourishes, "a modo de primavera de ilusión para las almas abatidas por la tristeza y la penuria" (140). Also to be noted in *Idolos* and *Sangre* is some tendency to refer to *almas* that are even more collective. In *Idolos* these are an "alma de un pueblo" (292), "alma de la ciudad" (359), "alma de aquellas comarcas" (359), and an "alma nacional" (292, 293, 295). In *Sangre* the references are to the "alma nueva de la colonia" (10), the "alma de las generaciones" (16), and the "alma de las multitudes" (48).

In *Idolos* an *alma* is sometimes attributed figuratively to non-human elements. This usually involves an element of nature--"toda el alma de la selva" (227), "el alma de un paisaje" (339), "la naturaleza imperturbable parece revelarse con un alma consciente y bondadosa" (372)--but a broken perfume bottle is said to be "exhalando toda su alma fragante y ligera" (365). The notion of a mystical "alma de las cosas," which will reappear in *Sangre*, where it is linked to the development of the plot, is introduced in *Idolos*. Here it is linked to the function of art when Alberto notes that "podemos vivir cien existencias sin entrever

35

jamás lo que un solo verso o una estatua puede revelarnos, en un instante fugitivo, del alma de las cosas" (239).

In *Sangre* the proportion of figurative attributions of an *alma* to non-human elements is greatly increased, and includes not only elements of nature--"el alma de la espuma" (6), "el alma . . . de la tierra andaluza" (13), "luminosa alma verde" (of the sea, 26), "alma del zafiro" (of the sea, 73)--but a wide variety of other elements. These include "el alma de la perla" (6), "el alma fresca y fugaz de algunas fuentes invisibles" (18), "el alma de sus proyectos de gloria" (28), "el alma de la danza criolla" (50), "el alma de la música" (63), "las maderas fragantes de Asia . . . con el alma de sus resinas" (73), and "el alma capitosa del vino" (78). The carefully selected furnishings in Tulio's Paris apartment have *almas* (30), and there is some emphasis on the *alma* of his ancestral home (16, 17, 34, 80).

The phrase "el alma de las cosas," although it occurs only once, has not only a figurative function but a structural one as well. Toward the end of the novel, when Tulio is totally dominated by the dream, Martí's extravagant statements about mermaids and the supernatural begin to make sense to him, seeming no stranger than his own experiences, and he takes them to be "frases triviales de puro conocidas o como rastreros modos más o menos justos, más o menos claros, de expresar el alma de las cosas" (76). In his *Camino de perfección* Díaz Rodríguez states that mysticism in literature is the "clara visión espiritual de las cosas y los seres," and that the mystic is he who knows "el alma de las cosas," this knowledge being the property of the poet and the artist (138). Although Tulio is not a poet nor an artist, he is the literary creation of a man who was, in a sense, both, and may be said to reflect his creator's views. In view of his all-encompassing fascination with the sea and its enigmas, suggested to him by Belén and the color green, his retreat into the dream and his ultimate suicide may be viewed as an effort to penetrate this mystery, or to finally understand "el alma de las cosas." [1]

In *Peregrina*, *alma*, the occurrence of which drops off precipitously, especially in comparison to *Sangre*, is almost never attributed to a non-human element. Rare exceptions include elements of nature, as in *Idolos* and *Sangre*--"el alma diáfana del agua" (117), "cambió de alma, aspecto y vida el paisaje" (185)-- and, unlike the earlier novels, animals. In the image cited earlier referring to Juan Francisco's talent for gentling young oxen, they are said to become "dóciles como una seda con alma" (97), and Amaro communicates with "el alma cándida y fugitiva de las bestias" (175). The use of the noun is clearly not only reduced in *Peregrina*, but narrowed, with primary emphasis being placed on the more literal connotations rather than on the figurative.

Belleza/Bello

The second most commonly occurring favorite words are *belleza* and *bello*, which occur most frequently in *Idolos*, and, perhaps unexpectedly, somewhat less often in *Sangre*. As in the case of *alma*, the use of *belleza/bello* drops off sharply in *Peregrina*. In all the works the substantive is more common than the adjective, and in *Idolos* and *Sangre* it is occasionally emphasized by capitalization. Related forms (*bellamente, bellísimo, embellecer, embellecido*) occur occasionally in *Idolos* and *Sangre*.

In *Idolos* beauty is quite often associated with women, either as a class or as individuals. During his travels, Alberto has seen "los más excelsos tipos de belleza de todos los países y todas las razas" (192), and he wants to create in the statue that will become his *Venus criolla* "la belleza del tipo de raza más común en el pueblo de su país, belleza original, mezcla de oro y canela, obscura y fragante" (220). The beauty of specific women, especially María Almeida and Teresa Farías, is also alluded to. For the young Alberto María "poseía la belleza irreprochable de las Diosas" (192), and there are a number of references to Teresa's extraordinary beauty (336, 337, 338, 340, 345, 364).

Belleza and *bello* are also associated with with elements of nature, specifically, the local landscape (173, 175, 227, 246), sunsets (324, 325), and flowers (189, 191, 248, 255), and occasionally with cities--Caracas (204, 346), Paris (265, 290), and the canals of Venice (202). In addition, the terms occur in such diverse images and expressions as "la cadena de oro de la palabra bella" (178), "con toda su belleza, en la belleza de la mano, sería como una gota de agua con todos los esplendores del Azul posada sobre un pétalo" (to describe a book, 198), "la vida de virtud, belleza y heroísmo del cumanés intachable" (General Sucre, 228), "expresiones y actitudes bellas y fugitivas (of people, 229), "el ministro . . . ensartaba frases y frases, algunas incoloras, algunas bellas, todas fáciles, casi todas vacías" (237), "es pérfido ese amor: da a las almas una gran belleza efímera, y las destruye en cambio" (249), "escribió un libro fuerte y bello" (275), "diálogos . . . pálidos, muy sosos, muy tristes, no encerraban la menor belleza" (282), "una palabra bella y luminosa de ciencia o arte" (293), and "un supremo acto de belleza" (370).

In *Idolos belleza* and *bello* are most often associated with the concept of art, often specifically sculpture. The association may be quite direct, as when artists are said to be "los más altos creadores de belleza" (222), or when statues are referred to as "figuras bellas" (187). But the association is often less direct, as in an image which refers to Alberto's nostalgic memories of his life in Paris: "siguió viendo hombres y cosas a través de los recuerdos, con sus ojos . . . hechos a la sonrisa, a la franca alegría de vivir, a las formas vestidas de belleza y a la belleza vestida de luces" (172). Alberto, after his discovery of art, is said to have been "olvidado en un éxtasis divino de belleza" (233).

37

Beauty, in fact, is sometimes conceived of as not only what the artist creates but as an intrinsic characteristic of the creator himself, or of those who appreciate the beautiful. Alberto, in his frustration at not being able to work effectively, perceives the *pequeñeces* of Caracas society as robbing him of "algo de lo mejor de su talento, de lo más bello de su alma y esencial a su vida" (229), and later, when he completes a statue and wonders what its reception will be, he realizes that artists must always have faith in their talent because this enables them to hear, "aun en los días áridos, brotar cantando en su alma la belleza como un manantial de aguas vivas" (266).

The notion of beauty is associated emphatically with the task of regenerating Venezuela, as conceived of by Emazábel and perceived by Alberto:

> Con humildad reconoció no haber soñado la obra tan grande ni tan bella como surgía de las palabras y del alma de Emazábel. . . . la obra aparecía derramando . . . tesoros de una belleza nueva, belleza militante, belleza heroica: la belleza de la acción, quizás más grande y seductora que la belleza de las obras de arte y la belleza de los sueños hondos e impasibles." (287)

For Alberto, and for Díaz Rodríguez, beauty is "multiforme." It may be perceived visually in works of art, in nature, or in women, but it may also be sensed as a sort of positive force which is continuously imperiled by the self serving interests of those who are unable to recognize it. In this last sense the notion of beauty is linked to the primary theme of the novel, the inability of the artist to survive in the hostile environment of his homeland.

In *Sangre* the idea of a *belleza multiforme* is also apparent, as is the suggestion of the power of beauty. The variety of elements and concepts associated with *belleza* and *bello* is smaller than in *Idolos*, but in this more concentrated approach the terms are more clearly linked to structure than they are in *Idolos*.

The most common association of *belleza* (never *bella*) is with Belén, whose almost supernatural beauty is emphasized at the outset and throughout the first chapter, which concludes with her death. In fact, there are no other uses of *belleza* or *bello* in this chapter, other than two references to "pseudo-*bellezas*;" that is, the kind of feminine "belleza vulgar" or "belleza mediocre" which moves some men to admiration when it is the only type at hand, as is often the case aboard ship (4). Belén's beauty, of course, stands in strong contrast to this type of beauty, or indeed to that of any ordinary woman. The word *belleza* does not occur in the first two paragraphs, but that the "presencia milagrosa" (3) whose effect on fellow passengers is "como un sortilegio" (3) is in fact a beautiful woman becomes clear when she is immediately compared to "una diosa del mar" (3). When her beauty is alluded to directly the allusion is a very forceful one: "Así fue que su aparición en la cubierta del buque . . . cayó en todas las almas como un rayo de belleza" (3). Díaz

Rodríguez is no more given to realistic description here than in the case of any of the characters of *Idolos* or *Sangre*, but the very modernistic passage that compares her physical appearance to elements associated with the sea provides a wealth of associations quite suggestive of physical beauty:

> . . . aquella novia . . . mostraba en su belleza algo del color, un poco de la sal y mucho del misterio de los mares. Bien se podía ver en su abundante y ensortijada cabellera la obra de muchas nereidas artistas que, tejiendo y trenzando un alga, reluciente como la seda y negra como la endrina, encantaron el ocio de las bahías y las grutas; al milagro de su carne parecían haber asistido el alma de la espuma y el alma de la perla abrazadas hasta fundirse en la sangre de los más pálidos corales rosas; y sus ojos verdes eran como dos minúsculos remansos limpísimos, cuajados de sueño, en una costa virgen toda llena de camelias blancas. (6)

The notion of beauty is also associated with Tulio's forbears, the artist and the nun-mystic, with whom, as has been pointed out, the colors white and blue, symbolizing beauty, art, love, and the ideal, are also associated, and who, together with Belén and the sea, represent the mystical quest that leads Tulio to his suicide. The association is quite clear in the case of the painter, who "nació a la belleza bajo el cielo granadino. El ambiente de harmonía y luz de la Vega lo inició en el misterio doloroso de la Belleza y del Arte" (12-13). It is less direct in the case of the nun-mystic, whose own physical beauty is mentioned: "Joven, rica y bella, se hundió en el recogido silencio del claustro. . . . el fresco lirio de su belleza fue poco a poco enrojeciéndose, hasta ser una sangrienta rosa expiatoria" (13). It is clear, however, that beauty is an aspect of the artistic/mystic element in the novel, and it is associated in some way with every ramification of this element.

There are several associations of beauty with Martí, the composer and musicologist, in whom the artist and mystic are fused ("Blanda luz mística bañó su fe y su arte," 51). He is "un creador de belleza" (47), and the fundamental laws of music which he has discovered in the Gospel will be promulgated "como solitarias cumbres blancas de belleza" (48). He creates "una música tan bella. Toda su música es bellísima" (66), and in fact his very soul is beautiful; his daughters' names "habrían bastado, por sí solos, a pregonar, como heraldos vestidos de armiño, el alma de belleza del padre" (62-63).

The epic/heroic quest is associated once directly with the notion of beauty: "La guerra forma pueblos, constituye naciones, hace la unidad y grandeza de las razas. Da vida, pan, oro y belleza" (21). The beauty of the epic/heroic element is strongly suggested in chapter three, as Tulio debates the merits of the pen, with which the term is directly associated, and the sword, and compares both to flowers: "Y el ideal, en aquella época obscura, tampoco florecería en cándidas imágenes de belleza, como un jazmín: daría flores como el rosal, en un incendio de púrpura. No rompería con timidez bajo la pluma, en cada palabra, como un azahar o una violeta: surgiría en el extremo de la espada con el triunfo de la rosa" (21).

Belleza and *bello* are also associated with other elements which are not tied to the plot. Many of these are the same as associations found in *Idolos*: landscapes (29, 70, 71, 75, 77), women other than Belén (18, 32), flowers (31), people ("almas bellas," 14), cities (Córdoba, Sevilla and Granada, 54), houses (15), and a few things that do not appear in *Idolos*, such as the "botín de belleza" of the sea (26), or the beauty of certain supernatural beings (85).

Belleza and *bello* persist in *Peregrina*, but their frequency, as well as their impact, is greatly attenuated. In fact, the terms, which occur much more rarely than in the earlier novels, almost always refer to the beauty of women, usually Peregrina (125, 156, 173, 177). Beauty is occasionally associated with Amaro--his eyes (176), and the "pensamientos de belleza y bondad" (197-98) that he retains after Peregrina's death. Bruno's perfidious words of love to Peregrina are once said to be "bellas" (184). But this is the extent of the gamut of associations. Even a linking with natural elements, which might be expected, is not found, suggesting that to Díaz Rodríguez the terms had a predominantly symbolic function and that there was thus no significant role for them to play in a non-symbolic novel such as *Peregrina*.

Ensueño/Sueño

Ensueño and *sueño* are the third most frequently occurring "favorite" words. *Sueño* occurs very frequently in *Sangre*, in which about half of the time it refers in a very literal sense to Tulio's dream, and therefore does not constitute a true "favorite" term. *Sueño* sometimes refers literally to dreams in *Idolos* as well, and in both novels *sueño* is occasionally used to refer, in a literal sense, to sleep. But much more frequent than these uses, especially in *Sangre*, is the figurative linking of *sueño* or *ensueño* to other notions. This device occurs almost twice as often in *Sangre* as in *Idolos*.

In both novels the most common associations made are with the notions of patriotism, art, and love, but these associations are often considerably more complex in *Sangre* than they are in *Idolos*, and furthermore are sometimes linked to structural elements in *Sangre* in a more complex manner than is the case in *Idolos*.

Sueño is first linked to the notion of patriotism in *Idolos* in a reference to Alberto's reactions to Emazábel's ideas and plans for the redemption of Venezuela at one of the early meetings of the "camaradas de 'ghetto'": "Soria acogió las ideas y los proyectos de Emazábel . . . como si las palabras de Emazábel no hicieran sino desvanecer las brumas de un rincón de su alma, o evocar en su alma las figuras dudosas y los contornos indecisos, vagos, confusos, de un antiguo sueño" (286-87). The association reappears toward the end of the book, as will be noted below.

The association of *sueño* with art in *Idolos* is usually with Alberto's profession as an artist, or in references to his artist friends, such as José Magriñat, who invites Tulio to accompany him on "uno de sus mejores sueños de artista, el viaje de Italia" (182), or the unfortunate Sandoval, who with the suspension of support from the Venezuelan government "cayó de su más alto sueño, de su aspiración más alta; pero cayó como artista, esforzándose por conservar en su caída un poco de arte y belleza" (270, see also 271).

When the association is made in the case of Alberto's own profession, it is usually juxtaposed with some allusion to the notion of love, and *sueño* is also linked to the notion of love when no overt connection to the notion of art is made. When Alberto leaves Paris to return to Caracas, he leaves behind him "muchos sueños de artista y el amor y los labios de Julieta" (188). His adolescent attraction to María Almeida was a "débil sueño de amor" (192), and as his more mature love for her develops the flowers he gives her are compared to his emotions and his attentions to her in an image in which *ensueño de artista* is an element: "de ese rincón de su alma, que no del jardín, venían los manojos de jazmines y rosas, y con esos ramilletes, otros ramilletes mejores, más frescos, más puros, hechos con ternezas de amante y ensueños de artista" (248). María's impression of him just before the passage in which her love is said to be blue, is that he "pareció venir de muy lejos, de muy alto, como de un ensueño remoto" (249).

As his relationship with María begins to deteriorate, Alberto percibe that the *sueño de arte* and the *sueño de amor*, which had not been in conflict within him previously, now are: "comenzaba sin causa aparente el divorcio de sus ensueños de arte y de amor, hasta ese punto unidos en un solo ensueño confuso y vago" (266). María also perceives a change; Alberto's words "ya no eran la música del corazón venida a cantar en los labios, como un enjambre loco y harmonioso de esperanzas y de sueños" (296). By the time Alberto's relationship with Teresa is fully developed, the *sueño de amor* has acquired strongly negative overtones and is perceived to be in direct conflict with the *sueño de arte* as well as with Alberto's dreams of redeeming his country, the *sueño heroico*. The enchantment Teresa exerts over him is compared to a *soplo*, emitted by every pore of her skin, and "a su ímpetu huían tímidos y desbandados los sueños: así los blandos sueños incubadores de bellezas como el gran sueño heroico de la redención patria. En el taller y en el artista no quedó sino el turbio y agitado sueño de la embriaguez voluptuosa" (339).

In *Idolos* the *sueño de arte* and the *sueño de amor*, although they are initially perceived to be a single entity and eventually to be in conflict with one another, are nonetheless at all times clearly defined. In *Sangre*, on the other hand, they acquire dimensions that blur the distinction between them, and at the same time relate them more closely to the structure of the novel. In addition, the *sueño heroico* receives different treatment.

41

It will be recalled that a link between *ensueño* and art is made in *Sangre* when Tulio's artist ancestor is said to be one of only two members of his family who "penetraron el secreto de la miel escondida en la copa insondable y azul del ensueño" (12), the other one being the nun-mystic. The artist's life was spent in Andalucía, "soñando sueños imposibles como los de un califa insano y voluptuoso" (13), and the nun's life, in an even clearer association, is said to have been "como un solo sueño" (13), and she herself "era un sueño que pasaba" (13). It is clear that the artist and the nun represent facets of a single concept, and that, as has been suggested earlier, this concept is Díaz Rodríguez' notion of literary mysticism, or the "clara visión espiritual de las cosas y los seres," which Tulio's suicide may be viewed as an attempt to attain. In the second chapter, a flashback of Tulio's life before his exile, he wonders whether it is his destiny to revive and continue the artistic/mystical tradition established by his two forbears:

> Ningún otro Arcos probó el suave martirio del sueño, después de la santa y del artista. Y la capacidad para el sueño, sin empleo ninguno, había venido tal vez acumulándose, reservándose en el seno obscuro de la raza, hasta romper en él, Tulio, como una rica vena de agua impetuosa. Así, en vez del héroe, como lo quería y admiraba él, quizá le tocase realizar el tipo de héroe más humilde, quizá le tocara ser un miserable héroe del sueño. (13)

At this point the *sueño artístico/místico* is in conflict with his compulsion to be not "un miserable héroe del sueño" but rather a hero in the tradition of other forbears who were *conquistadores*, and it is this option that he decides to take.

The phrases *sueño heroico* and *sueño épico* do not appear until later, when this *sueño* has come into conflict with Tulio's *sueño idílico*, his imaginary submarine wanderings with Belén. However, it is clear that there are always two types of *sueño* at war within him--the epic/heroic, which gains the upper hand temporarily on two occasions, and the artistic/mystic/idyllic, which develops into the mystical quest that dominates him in the end. Ocampo hopes that Tulio's return to Venezuela in response to his comrades' appeal, "renovando y exaltando su antiguo sueño heroico, tal vez lo movería a la acción y al combate" (80), thus curing him of his neurotic malady, but the fascination of the mystery represented by Belén and the sea (and later the mysterious mermaid who lures him to his death) is too strong for him to resist, and "mientras por los ojos de Tulio se entraba libre y señera la fascinación de la mar, Tulio dejaba el sueño épico, para acogerse al blando sueño idílico" (81, see also 90).

The phrase *sueño de arte* is also used to refer to the profession of Martí, whose wife, "consciente compañera de artista, protegió su vivo sueño de arte" (49). Martí's *sueño*, like Tulio's, is artistic/mystic, but, in sharp contrast to Tulio's indecision, Martí's life is characterized by a constant exercise of will. It

42

is, in fact, the epitome of single-minded devotion to an ideal, and in this facet of its nature his dream may also be said to be heroic, although the association is not made explicitly, and the heroism is not patriotic but rather refers to an inherent characteristic of Martí's nature. The concepts of heroism and dream are also linked in a reference to the nun's life, which , as noted above, is said to be "un solo sueño" (13); it is also likened to "un sueño largo y un largo beso . . . sueño y beso fijos, con fijeza heroica, hasta el último aliento, en los pies del Crucificado" (13).

In both *Idolos* and *Sangre sueño* occurs occasionally in personifications: "claro sueño de una fuente" (*Idolos* 244), "los vanos sueños de la planta" (*Idolos* 255), "el sueño azul de los pozos" (*Sangre* 53), and "el sueño de la onda" (*Sangre* 71). Although these are not linked, at least very closely, to the primary figurative associations, they do intensify the non-literal function of the terms.

The use of *sueño* and *ensueño* in *Peregrina* is markedly different. *Sueño* is never used in any but a strictly literal sense, to refer to sleep, or in one case to Peregrina's dreams, which are invaded by the fear that she may be pregnant (156). *Ensueño* occurs rarely, and always refers to an illusion or fantasy, but these are of course not the noble aspirations to art and patriotism held by characters of the earlier novels.

In fact, there are only two *ensueños* in *Peregrina*. One is a fantasy that appears to be a sort of substitution for a *sueño artístico* in José de Jesús, the stone-mason, who is "de imaginación fresca y virgen, pero falto de la indispensable disciplina para hacer de su oficio, con semejante imaginación, cosa noble y excelente" (138). He therefore creates a fantasy life which revolves around his conviction that he is surrounded by buried treasures, waiting to be discovered, and he manages to convince several other characters that his dream is a reality (139, see also 141, 142). The other *ensueño* is Amaro's fantasy of sharing a *rancho* some day with Peregrina (176, 177), an illusion which is shattered by his discovery of her relationship with Bruno.

The tendency to establish a dichotomy between different types of dreams that is quite evident in *Idolos* and *Sangre* survives here, although much less forcefully and with no connection to the essential plot. Rather the illusions are seen simply to be in contrast, and if either of them is noble, it is quite clearly Amaro's. José de Jesús' "perenne ensueño era como el desenfrenado desfile de riquezas quiméricas de un cuento de las *Mil noches y una noche*" (139), while Amaro's illusion is quite the opposite:

> . . . así iba él . . . labrando y magnificando la fantástica arquitectura del ensueño, hasta darle trazas y proporciones conformes con su ideal, no las de mágico palacio empedrado de pedrería como en un cuento árabe de *Las mil noches y una noche* . . . sino las modestas aunque para él suntuosas de un rancho semejante al viejo rancho de Ursula." (176)

Voluptuosidad/Voluptuoso

Díaz Rodríguez' preoccupation with *voluptuosidad* and *voluptuoso* (the substantive sometimes capitalized for emphasis) is far more apparent in *Idolos* than in either of the other novels. The terms occur roughly three times as often as in *Sangre*, and five times as often as in *Peregrina*, and the range of contexts is greater in roughly the same proportions. There is also a progression or development in *Idolos* in the contexts in which the terms occur that parallels the development of the plot, which is not apparent in *Sangre* or *Peregrina*.

Although the terms are usually used to refer to some aspect of physical passion, this is not true of the earliest occurrences, in which the association is usually with certain emotions of the protagonist, or in one case with a natural phenomenon. Early in the novel *voluptuosidad* occurs once in connection with Alberto's awakening appreciation of art. As he contemplates the possibility of an artist completing some of Michelangelo's unfinished work, he becomes obsessed with the idea, which "lo persiguió, lo dominó, lo poseyó, como una imagen de voluptuosidad a un débil cerebro de eremita" (183). *Voluptuosidad* is also associated with the pain and pleasure of travelling and returning: Alberto "se explicaba la inquietud de ciertas almas que, en un ir y venir alternado y continuo se procuran a cada paso el dolor de la partida y el placer del retorno, hasta hacer de la propia existencia una sola voluptuosidad triste" (197). Both terms are used to describe the pleasure Alberto feels when, in Paris, where he is an unknown, he is able to savor the knowledge that he might be a great artist, without having to prove anything, which is not possible in Caracas, where he is well known:

> . . . saboreaba la orgullosa alegría de no conocer a ninguno de aquellos seres que pasaban y de no ser conocido de ninguno, la voluptuosidad intensa y rara de sentirse solo, muy solo en medio de la multitud, alegría y voluptuosidad bajo las cuales llegaban a extinguirse las vibraciones y asperezas dolorosas de su alma, . . . Pero esa alegría voluptuosa . . . no estaba a su alcance en la ciudad natal, ciudad pequeña, en donde conocía a casi todos y era de todos conocido. (230)

Voluptuoso is an element of a very provocative image describing a sunset in Paris: "la luz de un día de primavera agonizaba en el cielo con lentitudes voluptuosas" (184).

To this point, all the associations in which the terms are used are more suggestive than they are precise, and the connotations are quite positive. As Alberto's relationship with María begins to sour the terms are associated with his unreasonable jealousy, and acquire more negative connotations, which although still somewhat vague have sexual overtones.

44

Just after he has seen María chatting with another man at a ball, the sight of another couple engaged in the same activity suggests to him "una visión parecida a las visiones locas de voluptuosidad y pecado que torturan el alma de un amante o de un esposo al germinar de la sospecha" (236, see also 237, 303).

It is in the fourth and final part, which is dominated by Alberto's obsession with Teresa, together with the themes of his progressive inability to work and his conviction that in any case his work will remain unrecognized in his native country, that some two-thirds of the occurrences of *voluptuoso* and *voluptuosidad* occur, and virtually all of them are linked to these elements of the plot. The sexual overtones become quite clear, and the connotations increasingly negative.

The attraction Teresa exerts over Alberto is quite different from the chaste allure of María (with whom the notion of voluptuousness is never associated). He first perceives it as a sort of pleasurable intoxication: "Su extravío y aturdimiento eran a veces tales, como si por cada uno de los poros de su cuerpo entrase, quemándolo y mareándolo con sus llamas y canciones, una voluptuosa embriaguez desconocida" (327). The concept of voluptuousness is most often used, and with the greatest sensual impact, with reference to Teresa herself. Her hands, for example, "flores de carne, esparcían voluptuosidad, que es el aroma de la carne" (340). The sensual aspect of her dual nature is repeatedly associated with the voluptuous, but voluptuousness is also associated with her excessive piety; the atmosphere of the cathedrals she visits during her pious periods awakes in her sensations that are "entre voluptuosas y místicas" (336). In a very forceful image that appears twice, the voluptuous aspect of her nature acquires a life of its own: ". . . y bajo su piel blanca se dormían sus voluptuosidades, como un rebaño de corzas bajo la nieve" (331). In the second occurrence of the image the latency established by the comparison with sleeping does acquires a force bordering on violence:

> Alberto asistió a un despertar de las voluptuosidades dormidas, bajo la blancura de Teresa, como un rebaño de corzas bajo la nieve. Dormidas durante su vida mundana, que en Teresa venía a ser la vida menos artificial, sus voluptuosidades un día, al roce más leve, al suave olor del incienso, despertaron de su blando sueño de corzas convertidas en tropel de leones ávidos. (337)

The concept acquires even more force as Alberto begins to imagine that in possessing Teresa he possesses "en vez de una simple criatura voluptuosa, la Voluptuosidad misma, toda la voluptuosidad, con su placer y su dolor" (340-41). Although this idea pleases him at first, it is not long before he realizes that in fact it is he who is possessed, by a force which extends beyond his obsession with Teresa, and which will finally destroy him as an artist:

. . . su fiebre, su gran fiebre de voluptuosidad, no se extinguiría bajo los besos del amante; con más furia, al contrario, seguiría dominándole, poseyéndole, incendiándole; continuaría alimentándose de cuanto en él había de más noble y puro: razón e independencia de hombre, y entusiasmo y genio de artista, para no dejar al fin dentro de él sino lo que deja toda fiebre, lo que deja todo incendio: pavesas, ruinas, despojos. (341)

Alberto's *fiebre*, as has been pointed out earlier, parallels the heat and dryness of the land, symbolized by the vivid red of summer foliage and the insistent song of cicadas, the symbol finally being condensed into the flames of the *roza*. As Alberto contemplates these flames the parallel is further extended to include Venezuela itself, which is a victim, as he is, of a malevolent force portrayed as both cruel and voluptuous:

. . . creyó ver la explicación de la última época de su vida, creyó ver la explicación de la vida alborotada de las gentes de su país y creyó penetrar el secreto del alma de aquellas comarcas, triste, ardorosa y enferma. Las purpúreas coronas de llamas de la roza eran las únicas dignas del dios de aquellas comarcas, un dios indígena semibárbaro y guerrero, cruel y voluptuoso, un dios que fuera al mismo tiempo el dios de la Voluptuosidad, la Codicia y la Sangre. (359)

At this point it might almost be said that *la Voluptuosidad* personified has become the antagonist of the novel, embodying the negative elements that Díaz Rodríguez perceives as obstacles to the development in Venezuela of art in particular, and to enlightenment and progress in general. That the words *voluptuoso* and *voluptuosidad* appear so much more commonly in *Idolos* than in *Sangre*, in which the element of political-social criticism is greatly reduced in importance, or in *Peregrina*, in which it can scarcely be said to play a role, is thus not surprising.

The terms also appear frequently in another key scene. Although the author's final message is expressed in Alberto's bitter "FINIS PATRIAE," the scene in which María verifies his betrayal of her epitomizes very eloquently the victory of the negative over the positive. As she enters the boudoir adjoining Alberto's studio, the first thing she notices is a "perfume de voluptuosidad" (365), an aroma which, as has been noted earlier, is elaborated on at some length, suggesting very forcibly the odor associated with the sexual act. María reacts not by feeling that her intrusion has defiled something good and beautiful but that she herself has been "violada por aquella atmósfera y su espíritu voluptuoso" (365). The violent outburst that follows must be viewed as a normal reaction to a situation that would provoke anger in most women, but the association of her feelings of degradation with the notion of voluptuousness, a notion which is never associated with her relationship with Alberto, and which has acquired quite negative connotations at this point, does lend itself to a symbolic interpretation.

46

Of the few occurrences of *voluptuosidad* and *voluptuoso* in *Sangre* only two have sexual overtones and both of these associations lack the intense sensuality noted in *Idolos*. Indeed, the association is quite tenuous when it occurs as Tulio's underwater idyll with Belén nears its end: "en Sorrento, su idilio volvió a ser tímido y casto, olvidándose del beso, cual si de un todo se hubiera quemado, en el viaje, el grano de voluptuosidad extraterrestre de donde la flor del beso había surgido" (77). Sensual overtones are somewhat more intense when Tulio asserts of his imaginary mermaid that "me abrasa en una voluptuosidad incontenible" (91).

The terms are associated twice with art, via Tulio's forbear the painter, who "enfermó de la tristeza y de su voluptuosidad, hasta morir en ese mismo paisaje, soñando sueños imposibles como los de un califa insano y voluptuoso" (13). *Voluptuoso* is linked once to music and Martí who, wandering through the Antilles, "sorprendió el alma de la danza criolla, alma de fuego, voluptuosa y esquiva" (50), and once, in a very imprecise but suggestive manner, to the notions of beauty, dreams, and love, in a reference to the Guadalquivir, "esperezándose y retorciéndose, más allá de los Molinos, bajo el cielo diáfano, como un sueño de amor voluptuoso" (54).

In all cases the terms have positive connotations. Whatever attraction the voluptuous exerts over any character is benign, if seductive (with the possible exception of the voluptuousness awakened in Tulio by his mermaid, which might be viewed as negative, since she will lure him to his death). The words cannot be said to be linked in any significant way to structural elements; certainly not as they are in *Idolos*.

It is clear that at the writing of *Peregrina* Díaz Rodríguez still retained some fondness for *voluptuosidad* and *voluptuoso*, but he does not use them often and their function is reduced to a single association. Each term occurs twice; the associations are always with the sensual, and are faintly reminiscent of some associations made in *Idolos*, but in their benign overtones they are more akin to those of *Sangre*. Peregrina has a "cuerpo de ámbar, en que despertaba la voluptuosidad como un perfume" (155), but she is no Teresa Farías. Her voluptuousness, in fact, is as pure as Teresa's is treacherous; in an image used twice to refer to her succumbing to Bruno's insistent demands, she is compared to "una bestezuela voluptuosa" (120, 132). Their relationship is once compared to "inúmeros collares de la voluptuosidad forjados caricia a caricia y beso a beso" (150).

One might wonder, given the fact that the relationship between Peregrina and Bruno is quite as physical as that between Alberto and Teresa, why the words do not appear more often, at least in this context. The rarity of their use, and especially the benignancy of the association is, in fact, in accord with the general tendency of Díaz Rodríguez to idealize in *Peregrina*, in spite of its *criollista* content, and to maintain some distance between himself and his characters.

47

Idílico/Idilio

Next in overall frequency of occurrence are *idílico* and *idilio*, which occur roughly five times as often in *Sangre* as in *Idolos*. *Idilio* occurs only twice in *Peregrina*. The terms are almost always used in the sense of "idyllic love;" there are only two occurrences where this is not the case. In *Idolos* Antonio José Sucre is said to be "el héroe del alma idílica" (228), and in *Sangre* Tulio perceives a "torrente de frescura idílica" as the dream begins to lose its terror for him (74).

The figurative association of *idilio* with *flor* or *rosa* is to be noted in both *Idolos* and *Sangre*. Alberto's adolescent love for María Almeida is a "frágil flor de idilio" (193), and when his later more mature relationship with her begins to deteriorate, he perceives the "rosas, hasta entonces blancas de su idilio, comenzar a teñirse de púrpura" (303, see also 310). In *Sangre* the metaphors, which always refer to ephemeral shipboard romances, are more imaginative, especially the one referring to "todos aquellos cuyo idilio floreció como una rosa de aire azul entre las jarcias" (81), and the one referring to Borja's belief that Elena Perales, whom he identifies as Tulio's romantic interest, "prefiere que su idilio se deshaga sobre el mar . . . como una flor de la espuma" (92). *Idílico* is also linked to *sueño* in *Sangre*, either directly, as in two cases when Tulio's *sueño idílico* is opposed to his *sueño épico* in the final chapter (81, 90), or implicitly, since most references to *idilios* occur in the descriptions of Tulio's dream.

The relatively stronger metaphoric impact of the use of *idílico* and *idilio* in *Sangre* is also due in part to the fact that the seductive power of Tulio's *idilio* over him is such that, by means of a sort of personification, it actually becomes an entity with which he wanders through the canals of Venice (75) and the Gulf of Sorrento (77), and which "se entretuvo tejiendo y destejiendo guirnaldas en vergeles maravillosos" (75).

Not surprisingly, in view of the overall conception of the relationships of Alberto with María and Teresa , on the one hand, and Tulio's with Belén, on the other, the *idilios* in *Idolos* are not totally idyllic. The *idilio* with María is consistently viewed as unstable: "frágil flor de idilio" (193), "aquella sombra caída en la riente mañana de su idilio" (296), and the image in which "Alberto vio las rosas, hasta entonces blancas de su idilio, comenzar a teñirse de púrpura" (303, see also 310). In the case of Teresa, in connection with whom the word is used only once, and with no metaphoric trappings, the *idilio* is "culpable" (330). In *Sangre* some *idilios* are also unstable, notably those shipboard ones referred to above; none are viewed as really blameworthy, and Tulio's dream *idilio*, besides being "tímido y casto" (77, see also 74), is completely idyllic, and stable to the point that it totally dominates him. Its effect on him may be said to be negative, but this interpretation cannot be based on any specific use of the terms *idílico* or *idilio,* which is always positive.

The change to be noted in *Peregrina* is again remarkable. *Idilio* occurs only twice, both times in non-metaphoric references. The *matapalo* tree, which has concealed the amorous activities of numerous couples, also protects Peregrina and Bruno, who "se acogieron también con la fiebre de su idilio al pie del matapalo" (149). The secrecy of their relationship is further protected by the dramatic effects conceived of and implemented by Bruno, and their "idilio . . . así, vivió largos días de impunidad perfecta y sabrosa" (153).

The fragility sometimes associated with the concept in *Idolos* and *Sangre* is not to be noted. This *idilio*, while it lasts, is very substantial, and although we know that it is fraught with guilt on Peregrina's part and is, with Peregrina, doomed, the word *idilio* itself has positive connotations. Its occurrence, albeit infrequent, is another example of Díaz Rodríguez' grafting of a modernistic device onto the *criollista* setting of *Peregrina*, which is itself idealized.

Diafanidad/Diáfano

In the use of *diáfano* (occurring once as *diafanidad* in *Sangre*), which is the least commonly occurring of the "favorite" words being considered here, a pattern that is rather circular emerges. The general type of associations that appear in *Idolos* reappear in *Peregrina*, although with about twice the frequency, whereas in *Sangre* the frequency is much greater and the range of associations wider.

In *Idolos* and *Peregrina*, both of which are set in Venezuela, the term is always associated with a natural element, specifically either some aspect of the atmosphere or an aquatic element. In *Idolos* it is used twice in metaphorical descriptions of sunsets, and reinforces the visual impact of shades of red. One image has been cited earlier: "A lo lejos, en Occidente, morían las últimas rosas diáfanas" (203). A second image refers to the dust of streets, that "se alza bajo las ruedas de los coches, y al pisar de los caballos, flota en los aires como nube, cuelga como un velo diáfano de los techos, refleja, suspendiendo así, la gloria purpúrea del crepúsculo muriente" (289).

One of the associations with an aquatic element describes the surface of pools: "pozos tersos, de cristales muy diáfanos" (328). A descriptive linking of an aquatic element with *diáfano* also figures in the other association, but in it *diáfano* is also linked to the notion of Maria's *alma*, which is "diáfana y pura como la onda" (298).

In *Peregrina* all the associations occur in quite striking images. One association is with an aquatic element and occurs in an extended description of the beauties of the Avila, which "por sus oquedades, frescas y profundas échase a discurrir perennemente el alma diáfana del agua" (117). The other associations are with the clarity of the atmosphere of the countryside, which is "diáfano y risueño" (153), and compared to "una gema diáfana" (158), and to a "diáfano y fúlgido bloque de cristal" (186).

That *diáfano* (once as *diafanidad*) should appear more frequently, and often with more complex connotations, in *Sangre*, the most modernistic of the three novels, comes as no surprise. As Holdsworth points out, these words were favorites of a number of modernists, who attached to them a variety of connotations.[2]

In only one instance is the association with the atmosphere--the "cielo diáfano" over the Guadalquivir (54). Associations with aquatic elements are more common. The waters of the Loire, flowing into the sea, "conmovían la ola: quebraban su cuerpo diáfano y empañaban su luminosa alma verde" (26), and in the final scene, immediately following Tulio's suicide, the sea "se extiende como un río y a los costados del vapor se dilata como un lago de oro, diáfano y rubio" (94). The mirrors Tulio chooses for his Paris apartment are compared to water: "Los quería . . . de cristales diáfanos, límpidos, como un agua pura" (30).

Diáfano is associated twice with imaginary or invisible sea creatures, and these associations are quite suggestive. Belén's hair is "como un alga rizada y obscura que trenzaron las ondinas con sus diáfanos dedos luminosos" (33). Toward the end of the book Tulio expounds on *lo maravilloso*, which he finds in the sea. He observes, "No es preciso ir a poner en un planeta lejano el reino de lo maravilloso. Lo tenemos bajo nuestros pies: en el mar, en cada ola llena de seres impalpables, diáfanos e invisibles" (85).

The most suggestive associations are with Martí, Tulio, and Tulio's dream idyll. Of Martí Díaz Rodríguez says that "la sinceridad lo envolvía como un arroyo diáfano" (46), and of Tulio, as he prepares to scatter flowers on the sea, Belén's tomb, that he "llegó a sentirse por dentro diáfano y profundo, como si la transparencia del agua se le comunicara a su espíritu. Se preparaba, con esa diafanidad interior, para el acto inminente, que había de ser sutilísimo y puro" (72).[3] The interruption of Tulio's idyllic dream by his comrades' call to arms is vividly suggested by the image "sobre el diáfano azul del sueño, abrió, como un alba sobre el mar, una rosa de sangre" (124).

As has been seen, the overall frequency of the "favorite words" is virtually the same in *Idolos* and *Sangre*, and it decreases markedly in *Peregrina*. Most common in all the novels are *alma* and *belleza/bello*. *Voluptuosidad/voluptuoso* is far more common in *Idolos* than in the other works. Although there are significant differences in the use of these and the other "favorite words" in *Idolos* and *Sangre*, not only are they more common in these novels, but their connotations and functions are more complex than in

Peregrina, in which, with their primarily literal or descriptive function, they appear for the most part as dim echos, stripped of their earlier suggestive force.

This is especially noticeable in the case of *belleza/bello* and *ensueño/sueño*, which in both the earlier novels have multiple connotations, and, especially in *Sangre*, a structural function as well, whereas in *Peregrina* the function is almost totally literal or descriptive. The use of *alma* in *Peregrina* also lacks the variety of connotations found in the earlier novels, especially *Sangre*.

The connotations and function of *voluptuosidad/voluptuoso* are most complex in *Idolos*, in which they are linked to the progression of the plot, from Alberto's initial innocent optimism to his final bitter disillusionment.

Idílico/idilio is also used in a more literal sense in Peregrina, whereas in *Idolos* and *Sangre* there is considerable variety in the connotations, which often appear in quite provocative images. *Idilios* in *Idolos* are either unstable or culpable; in *Sangre* (with the exception of some minor references) and *Peregrina* they are stable and positive.

Diáfano is always associated with nature in *Idolos* and *Peregrina*, and the context is always metaphoric. In *Sangre*, in which the context is also usually figurative, associations with nature occur, but the range includes further connotations, some quite modernistic. Both *Idolos* and *Peregrina* lack these more modernistic connotations.

NOTES

[1] See Matteson, "The Symbolic Use of Color in Díaz Rodríguez' *Sangre patricia*," (38-39). Debicki offers a similar interpretation when he refers to Tulio's dream as a "wider search for ideals" (62).

[2] It is interesting to note that Holdsworth cites Amado Nervo's reference to Díaz Rodríguez himself: "el indiscutible maestro del estilo, el dominador y conductor del idioma en América, el diáfano y hondo autor" (60).

[3] See Holdsworth for comments on the identification of *diáfano* with *puro* by some modernist writers.

CHAPTER III

SYNTACTIC DEVICES

As has been seen, Díaz Rodríguez' mastery of language is evident in two areas which involve the lexicon--the evocation of sense impressions and the use of certain "favorite" words. The reader will also note the use of stylistic devices at the phrase, sentence, and paragraph levels. Particularly evident is his fondness for what Persaud has called "the periodic sentence with branching arms" (238), and for the repetition of grammatical constructions, often together with conscious manipulation of their conceptual content, and in *Sangre* occasional expansion of the latter into syntactic motifs.[1] There is considerable blending of these two devices. Repeated grammatical constructions necessarily involve some "branching;" "branches" are often composed of repeated constructions, although this is not necessarily the case.

Branching Sentences

The "branching arms" usually consist of periodic bipartite or tripartite constructions within a sentence or paragraph, an inevitable effect of which is the creation of rhythmic patterns. Following are examples of these from each of the novels, given also in schematic outline:

> . . . la calle angosta, sucia, a un lado casi desierta y abrasada de sol; al otro lado, en sombra, algunos transeúntes; por la calzada, a trechos limpia, a trechos inmunda, un coche a todo correr y un carro lento, saltante y chillón. (*Idolos* 197)

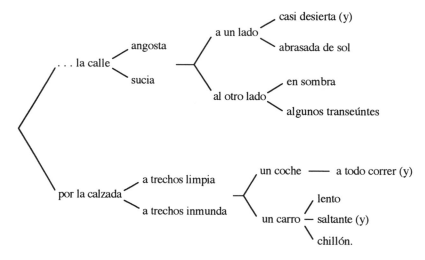

Ese perfume, olor de carne y esencia de besos y caricias, mezclado ahí a fragancia de flores y al perfume que María conoció por ser el perfume preferido de Teresa, llenaba la alcoba y parecía exhalarse del lecho y sus ropas y cortinajes finísimos, de las paredes, del tocador, y de todos los demás muebles de aquel rincón de taller convertido, por obra y gracia de la voluptuosidad, en *boudoir* elegante y deleitoso. (*Idolos* 365)

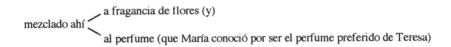

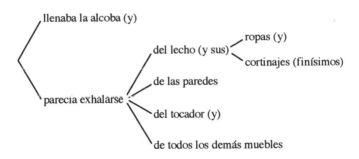

Huía de la chacota, del dicho vulgar, del hombre vulgar; y quería ver en todas partes actitudes y almas bellas. Tenía el entusiasmo fácil, y la justicia pronta. Su juicio, ya sobre cosas, ya sobre personas, era como un chorro de pasión, caliente y brusco. Ignoraba en sus juicios, como en lo demás, las encogidas atenuaciones y el cobarde término medio. Su alabanza era siempre llena y rotunda, como un aplauso estentóreo; y la censura partía de su boca silbando y rugiendo como un latigazo formidable. (*Sangre* 14)

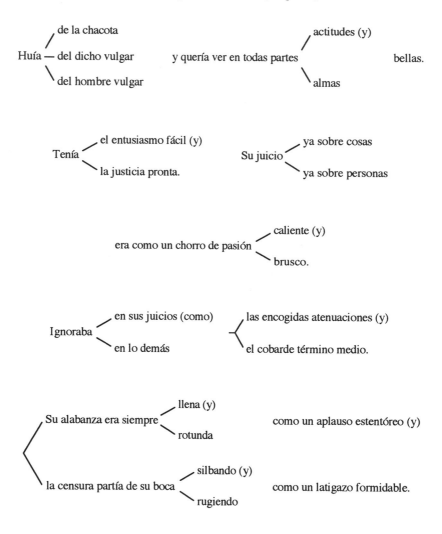

54

Algunos, los de alma poética, soñando y soñando, yendo y viniendo por obra y gracia de la fantasía, con el arte y la presteza de una leve araña hábil, entre el vapor y el horizonte lejano, labraban sobre las olas toda una complicada urdimbre de sueños vagos y azules. (*Sangre* 78)

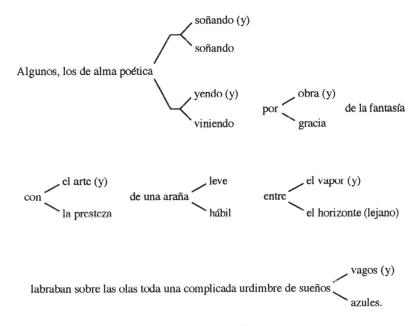

. . . se le antojaba con la vida tierna y frágil de quien se recobra apenas de una grave enfermedad, o con la vida suave y graciosa de la doncella y del niño, por sus dulces entrellanos o mesetas leves en declive y holgura; por sus repechos cuajados de lirios o anémonas; por los vagos tonos efímeros que el agua y la luz del cielo, según la hora y la estación, le dan, de claras amatistas o esmeraldas, de violetas o lilas, así se abrigue bajo el denso y cándido ropón de sus nieblas, o se eche por sobre senos y hombros el airoso velo de sus neblinas, o se recoja como tiritando detrás de la gasa impalpable de sus garúas. (*Peregrina* 117)

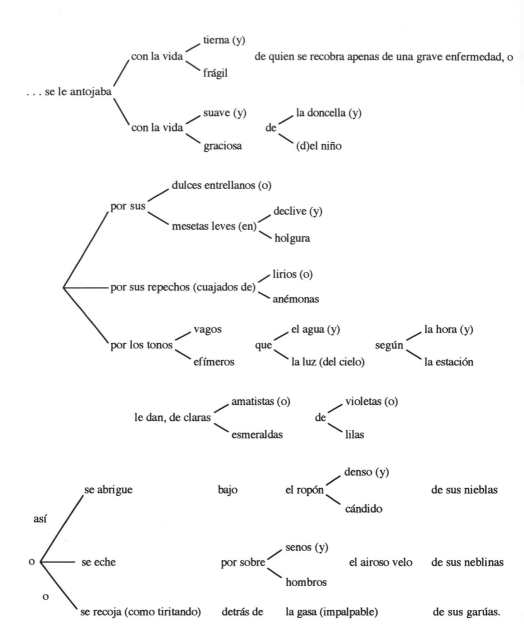

Malhallado con reglas y horas, con la necesaria subordinación a mayordomos y amos, poco a poco lo dominó y venció la nostalgia de la montaña y de la vida independiente, la nostalgia de su vieja existencia maravillosa, errabunda y libérrima de cazador de orquídeas. Alternadamente, su existencia discurría entonces en la montaña y la ciudad, y para ir y venir entre una y otra todos los caminos y veredas le eran buenos y todos eran suyos. (*Peregrina* 162)

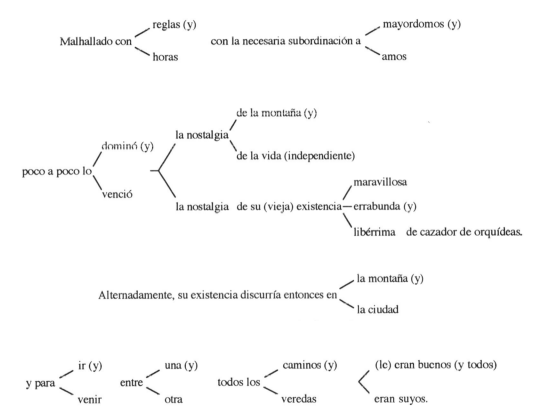

As should be apparent, Díaz Rodríguez' fondness for the "branching" sentence is quite intact at the writing of *Peregrina*. It is, in fact, one of the few devices studied here not to have undergone any diminution of frequency or effectiveness. If anything, it is more noticeable in *Peregrina* than in the earlier novels.

Repeated Grammatical Constructions

Repeated, or parallel, grammatical constructions, many examples of which are to be noted in the foregoing examples of "branching" sentences, are common in all the novels. In some cases the parallel constructions are grammatically identical:

> . . . estaba lleno **de silencio y abandono**, pero también **de inquietudes y tristezas, de dolor y hambre.** (*Idolos* 269)

> . . . pero ninguna de ellas **obscurecía como una sombra** ni **desfiguraba como una lepra** el nombre de los Arcos. (*Sangre* 18)

> . . . me la he pasado estos días, **de cañada en cañada, de sabana en sabana, de cerro en cerro** . . . (*Peregrina* 130)

More often, however, constructions which are clearly parallel are not grammatically identical:

> . . . **temerosas de ser profanadas,** y **desdeñosas de mezclarse** con la fealdad inquieta y vana de los hombres . . . (*Idolos* 183).

> . . . y la voz innumerable decía de tradiciones olvidadas y de glorias muertas, **a veces imperiosa como voz de conjuro, otras áspera como de reproche, o humilde y queda como de plegaria.** (*Sangre* 16)

> . . . **otras tenían figura de cerbatanas, otras apariencia de crótalos; otras eran trasunto de cigarrones cobrizos** . . . (*Peregrina* 118).

Especially evident in all three novels is the use of *ya* to introduce two, or occasionally three, parallel constructions. These also may be grammatically identical, although more frequently the parallelism is looser:

> Y Don Pancho, con voz **ya airada, ya lastimosa** . . . (*Idolos* 215)

Ya el cambio de aspecto de ciertas cosas le recordaba su larga ausencia,
ya la intacta fisonomía antigua de otras cosas representábale con tanta
viveza el pasado . . . (Idolos 172)

Los pasajeros, prontos al desembarco, pensaban en la tierra con interna delicia: *ya se*
veían paseando por las calles de la ciudad, sin el mareante balanceo de a bordo; *ya se*
miraban comiendo, alrededor de una mesa de restaurante, una comida algo diferente,
por lo menos, de la saboreada todos los días anteriores en medio de la promiscuidad no
siempre grata de la mesa común; *ya, sobre todo, se consideraban camino de un*
buen hotel . . . (Sangre 24)

Ya fue la reyerta en que se enredó una tarde con un hermano de Garzón en el juego
de bolos de la pulpería que da al camino real, junto al al mismo callejón de la hacienda. *Ya*
fue una serie de pendencias con que alarmó al vecindario del pueblo toda la
noche, y por las que el Jefe Civil dispuso arrestarlo. *(Peregrina 130)*

The primary impact of these parallel constructions, besides the creation of certain rhythmic effects, is
the intensification of the conceptual and emotive content of the passages in which they occur, but while the
reader will intuit this effect, he may not be aware of how it has been achieved. In some cases, as some of
the foregoing examples illustrate, the emphasis derives from simple reiteration. However, in many cases
the components have been carefully selected and the relationships between them consciously manipulated
in a variety of manners in order to achieve the intensification. In these cases the effect is, predictably,
more vivid.[2]

The latter type is very common in *Idolos*, and may be stylistically quite complex, involving, beyond
the iterative element which is readily apparent, various types of relationships between components.[3] Two
of them will be analyzed here.

A series of parallel constructions describes Alberto's state of mind immediately after he returns to
Venezuela from Paris at the beginning of the novel:

. . . siguió viendo hombres y cosas a través de los recuerdos, con sus ojos de cinco años
atrás, no habituados (1) *al llanto,* (2) *a la sombra,* ni (3) *al dolor,* sino hechos (4) *a*
la sonrisa, (5) *a la franca alegría de vivir,* (6) *a las formas vestidas de*
belleza y (7) *a la belleza vestida de luces.* (171-72)

59

Constructions 1, 2, and 3 show a parallel ordering into a conceptual class, here based on sorrow or sadness, as do 4 and 5, in which the class is based on the notion of happiness. Constructions 6 and 7 may also be said to be related, perhaps less directly, to the concept of happiness. Further parallelism is revealed in that *llanto* is a physical manifestation of *dolor*, as *sonrisa* is of *alegría*. There are three antithetical oppositions: *llanto-sonrisa*, *sombra-luces*, and *dolor-alegría*.

Constructions 6 and 7 also reveal another type of parallel relationship. Although *belleza* is reiterated, it has different syntactic functions, since in 6 it is the means or agent by which the action of the verb *vestir* is effected, whereas in 7 it is the object of the action of *vestir*. These different functions facilitate the notion that 6 is "modified" by 7; that is, if forms are clothed in beauty and beauty clothed in light, then forms must be clothed in light as well.

Another aspect of the antithetical structure of this passage is to be noted in its prosodic structure. When the constructions are viewed as a unit it will be seen that there is a certain progression from short, restrained, rather "basic" phrases to phrases which tend to be longer and which contain more communicative elements. An analogy to the musical terms *staccato* and *legato* might be employed to describe this contrast. When the semantic element is considered as well, the *staccato-legato* contrast creates the notion that the short, *staccato* phrases are to be dismissed rather quickly, whereas the longer, *legato* ones are to be dwelt on more at length. Such an effect is quite appropriate to the context, as Alberto has just ended his five year stay in Paris, where he was able to devote himself to the art he loves, and has reluctantly returned to his homeland, to family problems, to a corrupt government, and to considerable opposition to his chosen profession, all of which will give him reason to dwell, at some length, on his unfortunate circumstances.

The intensification of the emotional content of a passage is exemplified in two series of parallel constructions which occur in the long description of the physical aspects of Caracas during the dry season, and the metaphorical linking of these to the emotional state of Alberto as he awaits the arrival of Teresa at his studio:

> La tierra, en su fiebre, (A1) *con sus árboles atormentados de sed*), (A2) *con sus follajes ardidos,* (A3) *con sus florescencias rojas,* (A4) *con sus innúmeros cantos de cigarras,* no era sino un solo clamor que exigía del cielo inclemente la gracia de la lluvia. Así en todo él, como en la tierra febricitante, no había sino (B1) *un solo deseo,* (B2) *una sola ansiedad,* (B3) *un grito solo*: Teresa. (322)

Here the relationships are primarily those of parallel ordering, both within series A and B and between them, and of progression. In series A *árboles, follajes,* and *florescencias* are ordered into a class of visual images of plant life which is being consumed by the drought, as Alberto is being consumed by his passion for Teresa. The modifiers of these three nouns, *atormentados de sed*, *ardidos*, and *rojas*, all convey an impression of heat and dryness, which are the psychosomatic symptoms being suffered by Alberto as he awaits the arrival of Teresa. The *cantos de cigarras* evoke an auditory rather than a visual image, and the reference is not to plant but insect life. Nonetheless, particularly in context, the phrase contributes forcefully to the overall impression of fever and suffering, since earlier in the passage the sound of the cicadas has been said to be sharp, penetrating, strident, and deafening (321).

The constructions in series B are also ordered into a class. *Deseo* and *ansiedad* are both emotions experienced by Alberto as he awaits the arrival of his paramour. *Grito* does not, of course, usually convey the impression of an emotion; however, in context it probably may be understood to mean a sharp desire, or compulsion, to cry out.

There is a clear notion of progression in series B. Desire (for Teresa) becomes anxiety (that perhaps she will not come), and is finally realized as a compulsion to exhibit these emotions outwardly by crying out, perhaps as a means of relieving somewhat the tension he feels.

Alberto's *deseo* and *ansiedad* also bear a metaphorically parallel relationship to constructions in series A. The trees which are said to be suffering from thirst may be said to desire water, and the red and flaming foliage may suggest some sort of anxiety. In these parallels a visual aspect of the city is linked to an emotion experienced by Alberto. The parallel between the "innúmeros cantos de cigarras" (A4) and "un grito solo" (B3) is based on an auditory sensation which parallels, somewhat more indirectly, an emotion of the protagonist. The deafening song of the cicadas is a clamor which is aurally perceived by him, but which closely parallels the inner clamor of his emotions. These, furthermore, are perhaps on the verge of becoming an actual, audible *grito*.

Quite frequently parallel constructions in *Idolos* are separated by a number of pages. Three instances of this use of repeated passages, all of which refer to the sound of cicadas that dominates sections of Part IV, are suggestive of the motif device which will be refined and used to much greater effect in *Sangre*.

Each passage occurs twice, first in the introductory paragraphs of Part IV, which describe, against the background of the omnipresent sound, Alberto's emotions as he waits for Teresa in his studio, and then at a later point. Part IV opens with the sound of cicadas:

> Cerca y lejos, cada mancha de verdura, (A1) **cada rama, cada hoja,** (B1) **era un chirrido estridente, insostenible, como la nota más alta y gloriosa de una cuerda hecha de cristal que estuviese vibrando hasta romper de frenesí o de júbilo.** (321)

61

After a long flashback detailing the development of their affair and the events immediately following Teresa's arrival, the passage occurs again. Leaving his studio, Alberto goes to the Plaza Bolívar, as is his custom at that hour, and here the passage occurs at the beginning of the novel's most extended section devoted to criticism of the political situation:

> Arriba, (A2) *en cada rama, en cada hoja, una cigarra.* Y cada cigarra (B2) *era un chirrido estridente, como la nota más alta de una cuerda hecha de cristal que estuviese vibrando hasta romper de frenesí o de júbilo.* (346)

There is very little variation, the effect of the repetition resting primarily on simple reiteration. However, the omission of *insostenible* and *gloriosa* in B2 does create a reduction to the essential elements of the image--the comparison of the strident sound of the cicadas to a very high musical note--and this, together with the repetition in identical form of the remaining elements of B, is an effective reminder of the theme, particularly in the context of the other two repeated passages. The opposite approach, augmentation, is seen in A1 and A2, where the piercing sound is first associated directly with foliage, and then with cicadas in foliage. This creates a certain balance between the two passages, which reinforces the iterative effect.

The second repeated passage is more complex, both because of its length, and the accompanying context in the first occurrence. The first occurrence continues the initial allusion to the sound:

> De la escasa vegetación nacida a orillas de las quiebras y barrancos que, desprendiéndose del Avila, bajan a cortar y dividir caprichosamente la ciudad hacia el Norte, (A1) *venían los cantos monótonos y agudos*; venían del Oeste, de los raros follajes respetados aún por la incuria administrativa sobre El Calvario, colina antes revestida de flores y de lozana arboleda; venían de los cafetales tendidos al Este y Sureste de la población; (B1) *de todos los puntos del horizonte venían*; (C1) *y en la ciudad misma*, (D1) *de cada patio o corral lleno de árboles de sombra, de cada jardín, de cada plaza pública*, (E1) *surgía un coro idéntico ensordecedor y penetrante.* Y como en un grandísimo templo gótico van las columnas, los arcos y las demás partes del edificio enlazándose y fundiéndose de modo harmónico a rematar en la suprema esbeltez de la aguja, así (F1) *los cantos y los coros dispersos por toda la ciudad s e enlazaban y fundían en la atmósfera inflamada, sobre la ciudad ebria de bullicio y de sol, primero en un vasto coro unánime, y, por fin, en un solo grito desesperado que volaba hasta el cielo como un dardo impetuoso.* (321)

The passage is repeated at the end of the long section devoted to criticism of the political situation, as Alberto is forced to escape Caracas as a result of his brother's revolutionary activities:

(B2) *De todos los puntos del horizonte* (A2) *venían los cantos monótonos y agudos.* (C2) *En la ciudad misma,* (D2) *de cada patio o corral lleno de árboles, de cada jardín y cada plaza pública,* (E2) *surgía un coro idéntico.* Y (F2) *los cantos y coros, dispersos por toda la ciudad, se enlazaban y fundían en la atmósfera aun inflamada, sobre la ciudad ebria todavía de bullicio y de sol, primero en un vasto coro unánime, y luego en un solo grito desesperado que volaba hasta el cielo como un dardo impetuoso.* (358-59)

The variations occur in in the second occurrence, with the omission of *venían* (B2), the modifying phrases *de sombra* (D2) and *ensordecedor y penetrante* (E2), and virtually all of the accompanying context, the addition of *todavía* to F2, and the reversal of A2 and B2. The primary reason for the omission of *venían* is no doubt the contiguous placement of B2 and A2, which renders repetition of the verb unnecessary; omitting *de sombra* avoids identical repetition. The omission of the adjectives describing the sound, besides providing variety, tends to intensify the focus on the sound itself, which has already been said to be deafening and penetrating, attributes which are reinforced elsewhere in the section. Modification of *ebria* by *todavía* in F2, of course, emphasizes the continuing nature of the sound. The specific *puntos del horizonte*, identified in the accompanying context of the first occurrence (*Oeste, Este, Sureste*), are simply alluded to in the second occurrence, probably because a repetition of the entire passage was considered to be superfluous, if not tedious. But the phrase *de todos los puntos del horizonte* is significant, for it is also applied, at the beginning of the critical section, to describe the *politicastros* who come to the Plaza Bolívar, like the cicadas, "de todos los puntos del horizonte" (346). When they are identified as *senadores y diputados* a few lines later the comparison is repeated. This identification of politicians with the omnipresent cicadas reinforces the notion of the hopelessness of the political situation-- the incompetent, self-serving politicasters descend on the capital with the destructiveness of a plague of locusts. The placement of the phrase as the first element of the repetition occurring at the end of the critical section is an effective reminder of this link.

The two occurrences of the third passage surround the section detailing the relationship between Alberto and Teresa. It first occurs early in Part IV, as Alberto, awaiting the arrival of Teresa at his studio, hears the persistent sound of the cicadas, and imagines that it is the parched earth crying for water, as his parched soul cries for Teresa:

. . . Alberto, inactivo y solo en su taller, se imaginaba oír en aquel grito, (A1) *el grito de la tierra enferma de fiebre,* (B1) *torturada de sed,* que (C1) *clamaba a los cielos, implacablemente azules, por una gota de agua.* (321-22)

The passage is repeated at the end of the section, as Alberto once again succumbs to his unhealthy passion for Teresa; they enter the *boudoir* and surrender themselves to passion:

. . . confundiendo el grito de sus corazones insaciables y el impetuoso gritar de sus pulsos con el (A2) *insostenible clamor con que la tierra,* (B2) *torturada de sed,* (C2) *clamaba a los cielos, implacablemente azules, por una gota de agua.* (345)

Here again the two occurrences are largely iterative, the only variation being in A, in which the "cry" of the earth is given somewhat different emphasis. Element A1 repeats the *grito* found in the second repeated passage, and B1 repeats the modifier *insostenible*, found in the first repeated passage, which facilitates a psychological connection between the three. *Fiebre* (A1), is found frequently in Part IV to refer to Alberto's passion as well as to the figurative fever of the land, and its use here facilitates psychological integration of the passage into the wider context of the section. The use of *clamor* rather than *grito* in A2 reinforces the idea of the sound, since it conveys more readily than *grito* the notion of the participation of multiple sources (the cicadas) also suggested and reiterated in the verb *clamaba* (C1, C2).

Although the device is fairly ponderous and cumbersome at this point, these passages do constitute a sort of tripartite motif, integrated into the symbolic function of the sound, which emerges as a distillation of the anguish being suffered by both Alberto and his country.

Parallel constructions, many of which show some ordering of elements, are very common in *Sangre*. Two occur in a passage in the long flashback in the second chapter in which Tulio's family history is detailed. A very important part of this history, to Tulio, is his ancestral home, in which most of his forebears have been born and died. He considers the house, which has come into his possession, to be almost a part of himself, so thoroughly is it identified with his family:

(A1) *Cada ángulo,* (A2) *cada muro,* (A3) *cada fresco pasadizo* tenía (B1) *viva sangre de historia,* (B2) *hechizo azul de fábula* o (B3) *pálida fragancia de anécdota.* (16)

The ordering is simple, the constructions in series A referring to features of the house, and those in series B to the history of the family. Further ordering in series A is revealed in the choice of nouns, all of which refer not to the contents of the house, which we may assume have also been in the family for years,

64

but to features of the structure itself. This emphasis is maintained throughout the passages dealing with Tulio's obsession with the house. To him it is its hallways, patios, windows, pillars, and corners, all of which he assiduously protects from defilement or change, since they are so intimately linked to the family history. It is these physical features of the house that also acquire the imaginary voice which he perceives to be reproaching him for his inability to decide on a direction for his life, as indicated in Chapter I. At only one point is a piece of furniture mentioned, a marriage bed (16), but the emphasis is not on the bed itself but its position in the house. This does not mean that Tulio (or Díaz Rodríguez) is not interested in furniture. In the description of the Paris apartment there is heavy emphasis on furnishings (29-30). But the absence of this emphasis in the case of Tulio's family home facilitates filling the house with other things--the shadows and voices of Tulio's ancestors, and the essence of their history, to which the constructions in series B belong.

These constructions are ordered into a class that might be called "stories," which later context indicates come to Tulio through his great aunt. Their variety is indicated not only by the nouns (*historia, fábula, anécdota*) but the accompanying noun phrases. *Viva sangre* (B1) suggests the warrior tradition in which many of Tulio's ancestors engaged; the very modernistic *hechizo azul* (B2), and the synaesthetic *pálida fragancia* (B3) suggest the gentler occupations of other ancestors like the painter and the nun-mystic. Although these connections are not made overtly here, the notions are easily associated with the basic conflict within Tulio, which he will attempt to resolve first by becoming a revolutionary and finally by undertaking his artistic/mystic quest.

A series of parallel constructions with ordering occurs later in Part II, as Tulio ponders the antithetical nature of war:

> Cuando (A1) *parece destruir,* (B1) *construye*; cuando (A2) *parece empobrecer,* (B2) *acumula tesoros.* Como hermanas gemelas, de su pródigo vientre nacen (C1) *la gloria del capitán* y (C2) *la gloria del artista:* (D1) *el laurel* (E1) *tinto en sangre* y (D2) *la obra de arte* (E2) *vestida de candidez impoluta.* (21)

Constructions A1 and B1 parallel A2 and B2 grammatically, but the relationship between A and B is based on antithesis, the emphasis in A being on the negative, destructive aspect of war and in B on the positive and constructive. These antithetical relationships are quite clear from the vocabulary itself (*destruir/construir, empobrecer/acumular tesoros*). In the remaining constructions antithesis is noted between the two occurrences of each, although this is clear only when a wider context is considered. Military men (C1) and artists (C2) are not necessarily antithetical, nor are laurels (D1), associated here with glory in battle, and works of art (D2), nor blood (E1) and whiteness (E2). However, although it is not explicit here, and indeed would seem almost to have been absorbed into the single image of war,

Tulio's inner conflict, evident in the chromatic symbolism and elsewhere in syntactic devices in the section, can be seen to relate to these constructions as well, since the first occurrence of each is associated with the profession of arms and the second with that of the artist. Red (*sangre*) and white (*candidez*), normally not opposites, are also antithetical in this context.

With the use of syntactic motifs which are clearly integrated into the structure of the novel, the manipulation of parallel grammatical constructions in *Sangre* achieves maximum artistic effect. The motif device itself is greatly refined, and the integration far more comprehensive than is the case in *Idolos*.

One motif occurs in chapter II, when the reader is introduced to Tulio Arcos, his obsession with the notion that as the last male survivor of his formerly illustrious family he is responsible for maintaining its reputation, and his total inability to take any action in order to do this. The motif opens the chapter, and occurs twice in following pages, each time with slight variations:

(B1)   *"Un Tulio Arcos no podía quedarse viendo correr la vida como se queda viendo pasar el agua del torrente un soñador o un idiota."*   (9)

(A1)   *De ahí la reflexión abierta en su espíritu como una flor de orgullo*:   (B2) *"Un Arcos no podía quedarse viendo pasar la vida, como se queda un soñador o un idiota viendo pasar el agua del torrente."*   (12)

(A2)   *Y como una flor de orgullo, rompía de nuevo en su espíritu la misma reflexión*:   (B3) *"Un Arcos no podía quedarse viendo pasar la vida, como se queda un soñador o un idiota viendo pasar el agua del torrente."*   (14)

The three occurrences are largely reiterative, but there are significant variations both between them and within A and B. One of these is the extension of the second occurrence of A by the addition of *de nuevo* and *misma*, both of which emphasize the obsessive, persistent nature of the idea. The inversion of the two content components within A--the *reflexión* and the image *como una flor de orgullo*---also adds emphasis to the notion of the *reflexión*, since it is the first component mentioned, and the last.

The other interesting variations occur within B, the expression of Tulio's inner conflict. The change from the dynamic *correr la vida* in the first occurrence to the more passive *pasar la vida* in the second and third, suggests a decrease in vitality. This is in fact what has occurred in Tulio, who has participated actively in a revolution, but who at the beginning of the novel is in a state of complete *abulia*, unable to act or to make decisions regarding the direction of his life. He is in constant torment, but life passes, inexorably, like a torrent of water, and he stands passively by.

The variant position of the phrase *un soñador o un idiota* also contributes to the notion of a decrease in vitality in Tulio. In the first occurrence it is placed in final position, and thus stands in sharper contrast to the allusion to (Tulio) Arcos, which always occurs first. Its subsequent placement within the construction lessens this contrastive force and suggests that perhaps even the concept of similarity between his own attitudes and those of dreamers and idiots has become less distinct in Tulio's mind, and that thus the situation gradually seems to him less serious and the necessity to act less urgent.

A more complex motif occurs at fairly regular intervals in the final chapter:

(A1) *El mar, hasta perderse de vista, reía y retozaba con un continuo cabrilleo.* (B1) *Infinitos choques de olas diademadas de espuma simulaban, en azules praderas, el triscar de un rebaño infinito.* (C1) *Una bandada de gaviotas, de cuando en cuando, rayaba el cielo con una blanca y neta línea curva.* (77)

(A2) *El mar, hasta perderse de vista, reía y retozaba con un continuo cabrilleo.* (C2) *De cuando en cuando, una gaviota rayaba el cielo con una blanca y neta línea curva.* (81)

(A3) *El mar, hasta perderse de vista, reía y retozaba con su continuo cabrilleo.* (B2) *Infinitos choques de olas diademadas de espuma simulaban, en azules praderas, el triscar de un rebaño infinito.* (87)

As in the first motif analyzed, variations occur both between the occurrences and within them, and these variations are intimately related in the overall effect. Within C the progression from *una bandada de gaviotas* to *una gaviota*, together with the fact that C does not appear in the final occurrence, suggests quite clearly the gradual disappearance of the gulls. Within A, with the change from *un continuo cabrilleo* to *su continuo cabrilleo* in the final occurrence, the transition from the indefinite article to the possessive suggests that this aspect of the seascape is perceived first as something indefinite, perhaps even accidental, but that it is finally perceived as an established, constant element.

These two variations reinforce a more general effect, created by variations between the three occurrences of the constructions. It is immediately apparent that only A appears in each occurrence, and that B and C each appear twice, but not together except in the first. Schematically the distribution is:

67

1. A B C

2. A   C

3. A B

Construction A, which describes the sea in general rather than some specific aspect of it, as in B and C, is common to all three occurrences. As has been noted earlier, the theme of the sea and its attraction for Tulio is the predominant theme of the novel, and in this motif the sea, and more specifically the notion of the infiniteness of the sea, in space (*hasta perderse de vista*) and time (*continuo cabrilleo*), is given primary emphasis. The more specific aspects of the description of the panorama--the waves (B) and the gulls (C)-- do not appear in all three occurrences, and the distribution of these constructions with relation to A produces an interesting structure. Construction A is stable, eternal. The sea is a constant in time and space. Construction A, besides appearing in all three occurrences, is the first in each. Construction B, the specific appearance of the waves, is also a fairly stable element, and closely linked to A. Nonetheless, it is a more specific, more detailed, aspect of the panorama, which might not be noticed momentarily, as apparently is the case in the second occurrence, in which it does not appear. Construction C is the least stable--a flock of gulls is reduced to a single bird, which then disappears completely.

The progression ABC, AC, AB suggests that when one observes the sea, a constant element, one may also note more specific aspects of the panorama, the particular appearance of the waves crowned with foam, and the presence overhead of a flock of gulls (ABC). Later, although the sea, the constant element, remains the same, one's attention may be distracted from the particular aspects of it on noting that the flock of gulls has been reduced to one bird (AC). Still later, although the sea, with its waves crowned with foam, remains the same, one may note the disappearance of the only living aspect of the panorama, the gulls (AB). The dichotomy between the permanence of the world around us and the ephemerality of human life is inevitably suggested, and is consistent with the context, since Tulio Arcos will very shortly fling himself into the eternity of the sea.

The reiteration of the phrase *reía y retozaba* clearly suggests that another important feature of the sea, besides its permanence, is its indifference, and its resistance to attempts to penetrate its enigmas. This is, furthermore, the final impression of the sea in the book. Although the parallel constructions just analyzed do not occur again, nor does *retozaba*, *reía* does recur (90, 92, 94), creating the impression of a condensation, in this verb, of the essence of the sea, which in its superiority as the possessor of final answers laughs at the plight of man.

68

Parallel constructions appear quite commonly in *Peregrina*, and many of them show some ordering of elements. In a passage comparing the attributes of the two brothers the ordering is basically antithetical:

> Mientras Amaro, (A1) *grande, tosco, fuerte y serio,* evocaba la imagen de (B1) *un bloque de piedra, sin desbastar, desgajado de la cumbre,* Bruno, (A2) *ágil, pequeño, inquieto y nervioso,* era (B2) *la movilidad perenne del agua o de la ardilla.* (111-112)

In these constructions a series of four adjectives is attributed to each brother (A1, A2), and each series is followed by a comparison to natural elements (B1, B2). *Grande* and *pequeño,* and *serio* and *inquieto* are directly antithetical. There are no direct opposites for *tosco* and *fuerte*. *Agil,* however, conveys a notion that is conceptually quite, if not completely, opposite from *tosco,* and if *fuerte* is considered in the context of the other descriptive elements attributed to Amaro it conveys an idea not only of physical strength but of stability, permanence, and reliability. *Nervioso,* on the other hand, especially in the context of the other descriptive elements relating to Bruno, suggests instability, mobility, and capriciousness. The wider context of the novel, of course, indicates that these are in fact characteristics of the two men.

Amaro is compared to a block of stone, *sin desbastar,* conveying the double sense of uncut or unpolished stone, and uneducated or "unpolished" person. That this stone is part of the Avila is clear from the phrase *desgajado de la cumbre.* Amaro has been identified earlier with the mountain, and with other stable, constant elements of the countryside. At the beginning of the novel we learn that he has deserted the army and returned to his beloved native region, of which he feels an integral part (108). Bruno, on the other hand, although he loves the mountain, and in his repeated flights from army recruiters comes to know it like the palm of his hand, does not identify with it in the same way. To him it is a living being, separate from himself, from which he learns to value freedom (117). Fearful of any threat to his freedom he is almost constantly on the move, gathering orchids on the mountain and selling them in Caracas, evading recruiters, and finally even Peregrina, and it is quite appropriate that he be compared not to stable elements of the environment but to the "constant mobility of water, or squirrels." The use of *movilidad* has further significance, since, as we will learn later, Bruno's character, unlike that of his brother, is fickle and inconstant.

In a flashback inserted between Amaro's learning of Peregrina's situation from her father and his seeking out of Bruno, Díaz Rodríguez gives details of Amaro's life and personality, his love for his oxen, his mother, his brother, and especially for Peregrina, the latter never declared. In a second reference to this secret love two series of parallel constructions are employed, followed by three more which describe the characters of Peregrina and Amaro as the latter imagines them:

> . . . el secreto de su corazón . . . era tan grande que amenazaba sofocarlo, (A1) *ya resonando* dentro de él (B1) *a manera de una música*, (A2) *ya enflorándose y perfumando* (B2) *como un jardín* en primavera. Siendo ella (C1) *bonita*, (D1) *buena* y (E1) *hacendosa*, y él (C2) *fuerte*, (D2) *serio* y (E2) *trabajador* . . . (176)

The parallels here are fairly simple, all being based on conceptual classes. In series A and series B, which are quite modernistic, the verbs *resonando, enflorándose* and *perfumando* and the associated nouns *música* and *jardín* belong to the class of sense impressions. This association of Amaro, the "unpolished stone," with lyrical elements is not as surprising as it might seem, since quite early in the novel we learn that he does appreciate beauty. The entire second chapter, probably the most lyrical of the novel, is devoted to a description, in some detail, of a typical early morning in his life. The chapter abounds with allusions to the beauty of the countryside--the color and fragrance of flowers, the humming of bees, and the singing of birds--to which Amaro responds: "Y el corazón de Amaro se puso también a cantar, como otro pájaro madrugador, con toda la alegría del amanecer" (108). That his love for Peregrina should be likened to music and fragrance thus comes as no surprise; rather, the image serves to intensify the notion of his poetic nature, and its placement immediately after he learns that his love is impossible intensifies the reader's sympathy for him.

The nouns in series C, D, and E may be said to belong to a class of positive personal attributes. There is some further ordering in that *bonita* (C1) usually refers to an attribute that is visually perceived, as strength (*fuerte,* C2) may be as well; *buena* (D1) and *serio* (D2) are attributes of character, and *hacendosa* (E1) and *trabajador* (E2) refer to the specific characteristic of industriousness shared by Peregrina and Amaro. These characteristics have already been attributed to the two, but their reiteration here, particularly in parallel order, provides emphasis, and further intensifies the reader's sympathy, since we know that both of these good people have been victimized by Bruno.

Two repeated passages are somewhat reminiscent of the motif technique. One of these occurs first at the end of chapter III and again at the end of chapter V, although the first in fact occurs later chronologically than the second, the intervening pages being a flashback, part of the content of which is the development of the relationship between Peregrina and Bruno, which is well under way at the beginning of the book. The setting in which the passages occur is the same--the bank of the *acequia* that flows from the *pozo encantado*--and the earliest passage occurs as Peregrina first succumbs to Bruno's advances, and her own desires. Bruno, jealous of his brother Amaro, and still uncertain of Peregrina's love for him, throws himself on her, restraining her arms, and kissing and biting her neck. She resists briefly and then:

> . . .(A1) *desfalleció y cayó entre los brazos de él,* (B1) *pálida, trémula,* (C1) *entregada, como humilde bestezuela voluptuosa.* (132)

As she surrenders to him, she finally admits that she loves him.

The later passage occurs the day following the manifestation of the *encanto* and the subsequent discussion of *brujos* that opens the novel. Peregrina is waiting at the *acequia* for Bruno, and when he arrives she tells him that things cannot go on as they have; she is progressively more afraid of discovery. Bruno again restrains her arms, kisses her neck, and Peregrina responds:

> . . . (A2) *desfalleció y cayó entre los brazos de él,* (B2) *pálida, toda trémula, en un solo espasmo y deliquio,* (C2) *entregada como una bestezuela voluptuosa.* (120)

But here she begs him to leave her, and he obeys..

The differences between the passages are lexical; specifically, the use of *humilde* in C1 and its omission in C2, and the addition of *toda* and the phrase *en un solo espasmo y deliquio* to B2. These descriptive elements refer to other elements that are the same in both passages: Peregrina swoons and falls into the arms of Bruno; she is pale and trembling, and she surrenders to him as if she were a voluptuous little beast. What is different about the two episodes lies not in the action but in the reader's perception of Peregrina. In the first instance, which we may assume is her initiation into the pleasures of the flesh, she is still *humilde* (meek, modest, submissive). The emphasis, particularly in the context of her confession of love, is on her innocence, and the overall impression created is one of this innocence succumbing to a sensual compulsion that is powerful but not very clearly defined. In the second instance the compulsion is more precisely suggested by focusing more intensely on its physical manifestations. The addition of *toda* to *trémula* conveys more clearly the notion that her entire body is trembling. Even more effective is the addition of the phrase *en un solo espasmo y deliquio,* in which the nouns suggest quite forcibly the physiological sensations associated with sexual excitement. The overall impression here is that Peregrina is no longer innocent, but experienced in appreciating the pleasures of physical love. She is also more in control, as suggested by the omission of *humilde,* which is appropriate to the context of her begging Bruno to leave her, and his obeying.

In the other "semi-motif" passages the overall construction is looser, but there are clear grammatical and conceptual parallels. The passages are widely separated, the first occurring at the end of chapter II, the lyrical description of a typical day in the life of Amaro, his love of nature, and for Peregrina, and the second in chapter XII, in a short flashback which interrupts the episode in which he learns of Bruno's betrayal.

In the first passage Amaro is remembering his dead mother and the *rancho* where he grew up, now abandoned. His dream is to rebuild it for himself, Bruno, and perhaps "alguien más" (Peregrina), and he imagines it:

> . . . (A1) *con su corredor bien oreado por la brisa,* (B1) *donde en trípode rústica, sobre la indispensable hoja de plátano, reposaba el bernegal reluciente.* . . .Miraba sobre (C1) *la cocina del rancho, pulidísima y fresca, y siempre llena de buen olor, un penacho de humo.* Y dentro del rancho, donde Ursula tenía (D1) *una imagen de Nuestra Señora de las Mercedes o de Nuestra Señora del Rosario,* porque él ya no se acordaba muy bien de la imagen, miraba otra imagen de la Virgen. Gracias a la imprecisión del recuerdo, (E1) *su pensamiento substituyó la antigua imagen con otra nueva.* Sus *rasgos* puros y juveniles aparecen compuestos en la actitud *graciosa* de una sencilla cargadora de agua. Y Nuestra Señora, en el pensamiento de Amaro, se sonrió bajo el agua derramada de la tinaja llena, *con los labios, con los ojos, con toda la cara de Peregrina.* (109)

In the flashback which includes the second passage we learn that Amaro has come to take it more or less for granted that a simple indication of his intentions to Peregrina's father will suffice to make her his, but that his timid, reticent nature has not allowed him to verbalize his desires. Instead, he has internalized them, elaborating in this way his humble dream, in which he imagines his mother's *rancho*:

> . . . (A2) *con su corredor bien oreado por la brisa,* (B2) *donde, en trípode rústica, sobre la hoja de plátano, reposaba el bernegal reluciente;* (C2) *con su cocina, pequeña, pero fresca, pulida y empenachada de humo;* con la alcoba que hace de salón tapizada de grabados y cromos, (D2) *aquella estampa de Nuestra Señora,* en la que, mejor que el pincel de un Correggio, (E2) *la imaginación de Amaro viviera substituyendo, a los rasgos de la imagen sagrada, los ojos, la boca, la gracia y la belleza de Peregrina.* (176-77)

While there is some variation between the two occurrences of constructions B and C, these and A, which is repeated in identical form, express essentially the same content. It is difficult to attribute much, if any, significance to the omission of *indispensable* in B2. It may be said that the somewhat longer description of the kitchen in C1, which includes an olfactory reference omitted in C2, places more

72

emphasis on this aspect of the fantasy here. However, the import in both passages is that Amaro sees in the image of the Virgin, the most perfect of women, the object of his amorous desires, and that this is in a domestic setting. The psychological implications are clear. It is also clear that the process by which Amaro creates this fantasy, and the nature of the fantasy itself, have undergone some changes. These are expressed in the variations between the occurrences of constructions D and E, together with the accompanying contexts.

In the first passage the substitution of the figure of Peregrina for that of the Virgin is attributed to Amaro's inability to remember the image very precisely, and the psychological process seems to be almost subconscious. In the second passage his imagination "lives" on the process, suggesting that it has become more conscious, or at the very least much more vital to his existence.

In the fantasy itself there is an obvious condensation in the second passage, which is achieved not so much by manipulation of the parallel elements as by the omission of details in the accompanying context. The allusion to the possible exact identities of the Virgin is not repeated, nor is that to Peregrina imagined with a bucket of water on her head. The setting, too, although identical in both passages, is treated in a somewhat abbreviated manner in the second. The effect created by this condensation is to reduce the illusion to its most essential elements, which are the details that identify the *rancho* as Amaro remembers it, the identification of Peregrina with the Virgin and the accompanying psychological associations, and the details of Peregrina's beauty. The poignancy of the dream is somehow enhanced by this reduction to its essence, and that it should be evoked in this form at this point is appropriate to the wider context. It will not be mentioned again, and it has the effect here of reinforcing the impression of acute pain that Amaro feels on learning that it is, in fact, an illusion.

While it is obvious that Díaz Rodríguez retains some fondness for the motif device in *Peregrina*, it should be clear from the foregoing discussion that he no longer uses it with the control or the structural integration that characterize its use in *Sangre*. These repeated passages, especially the second one, are more reminiscent of the use of the device in *Idolos*.

As has been seen, "branching" sentences are very common in all three novels, especially *Peregrina*. Also common in all the works is the repetition of syntactically parallel constructions, within and between which elements may be consciously manipulated to intensify the conceptual or emotive content of the passages. The latter device reaches a peak in *Sangre* in which it is used several times to create recurrent syntactic motifs which are clearly integrated into the structure of the novel. This use of motifs is the significant syntactic feature in which the style of *Sangre* may be said to differ substantially from that of *Idolos* and *Peregrina,* in which the device is noticeably less controlled and effective.

NOTES

[1] Various critics have noted the use of motifs in *Sangre.* See, for example, Araujo 83-84, Debicki 64, Matteson, "Motivos sintácticos en *Sangre patricia,*" Olivares, *La novela decadente en Venezuela,* 114-15, and Woods 303.

[2] This device as it occurs in various periods of Spanish literature has been studied at some length by Alonso and Bousoño.

[3] See Matteson, "Syntactic Patterns in Díaz Rodríguez' *Idolos rotos.*"

CHAPTER IV

IMAGERY

The use of imagery is very common in all three novels, and perhaps more than any other element serves to create the *tensión lírica* cited by Anderson Imbert as one of the essential characteristics of modernistic prose (399). As will be noted in the following discussion, two characteristics of the figurative use of language are common to all the works: there is a marked preference for the simile, and many images involve sense impressions. There are, however, significant differences in the use of metaphor as it appears in the three works, specifically, in the relative frequency of its use (density), and in the degree of complexity of the images themselves.

Density

In both *Idolos* and *Peregrina* images are interspersed at fairly regular intervals among sections which are essentially prosaic. In *Sangre*, on the other hand, there are rather few really prosaic sections. On the contrary, it fairly abounds with imagery, and it is this density of figurative language which comprises one of the distinguishing marks serving to set off its prose style from that of the other two novels. The following passage, which describes the activity of Martí, is a good illustration of the density of imagery that is common in *Sangre*:

> Mientras ganaba el pan de su cuerpo con lecciones de piano a señoritingas obtusas, proveía al sustento de su espíritu en el hogar de su vida interior, cultivando y embelleciendo esta vida como un jardín cerrado. Con la savia de su juventud creaba flores y con éstas, de tiempo en tiempo, celebraba, en todo el ámbito de su jardín, la primavera de la música. Eran flores frágiles, trabajadas con la substancia inmaterial del sonido, vaga y efímera si el arte no la transforma en substancia dura y eterna. Algunas alcanzaban, perdurando, la más gloriosa fijeza artística. Y la mayor parte, sobre todo cuando el jardín, muy pequeño, no bastaba a su carga de flor, se desbordaban de él, en sonora lluvia de pétalos impalpables, a colmar la honda melancolía del violoncelo, a mitigar la perenne tortura del violín o a danzar por sobre las blancas teclas del piano, entre dulces discreteos amorosos. (47-48)

Passages with some density of imagery are found occasionally in *Idolos*. The following, which refers to the dialogues between Alberto and María as lovers, is probably the best example:

> . . . así, hermosamente, divinamente, de confidencia en confidencia, reconstruían la vida, desde el instante en que el amor entró en ellos, y en sus corazones floreció como un gran

75

lirio de luz alba. Cogidos de la mano, iban de recuerdo en recuerdo, como dos amantes niños, de corazones puros, en sendero bordado de margaritas, van de margarita en margarita, deshojando las estrelladas flores cándidas, entre dulces balbuceos deliciosos. Pero una vez, mientras deshojaban un recuerdo, de éste, como a improviso conjuro, surgió una sombra. Y ni esa noche, ni despúes, volvieron a deshojar, entre dulces balbuceos, pálidas margaritas ideales. (299)

True density of imagery is extremely rare in *Peregrina*. The following passage, which refers metaphorically to Peregrina's anguish as she reflects on the possible consequences of her affair with Bruno, is one of very few in which it does occur:

A través de su cuerpo de ámbar, en que despertaba la voluptuosidad como un perfume, su alma radió con un fulgor divino. Pero, al reflexionar en la más natural consecuencia probable de su amor, y decirse, loca de pánico: "¡si eso sucediera, qué vergüenza, Dios mío!", la encendida luminaria de su alma comenzó a declinar, a menguar, a bajar con bajada vertiginosa en una larga noche de pesadilla y de terror, tal como una luz que, despúes de ser en lo alto fanal radiosísimo, y tomando proporciones cada vez más pequeñas, de lámpara, de candil, de chispa microscópica, bajara, hasta apagarse, por un aljibe profundo en donde se hubiese refugiado toda la sombra del Universo. (155)

Complexity

The other distinguishing mark, and an even more significant one, which serves to set off the prose style of *Sangre* from that of the other two novels is the fact that in general its imagery is considerably more complex.

Some degree of complexity is a natural consequence of density itself when, as is the case in all the above passages, there is extension of particular metaphors throughout the passage, and further elaboration of the elements of these. In the passage from *Sangre,* for example, the basic comparison is between music and flowers. From this metaphor two further comparisons are derived: *primavera de la música,* which likens the creative activity of the composer to the creation of plant life which occurs in the spring, and *sonora lluvia de pétalos impalpables*, which compares the musical compositions that are never set down, and which therefore may never again be sensorially perceived, or audible, to petals which cannot be sensorially perceived, or touched. The *jardín* image also derives from the element of flowers. The basic metaphor in the passage from *Idolos* is the comparison between love and flowers. It extends throughout, and these elements are further elaborated in a shift to more specific aspects of each--the memories of the lovers and the petals of daisies. The passage from *Peregrina* is based on the metaphorical comparison between Peregrina's being and light, and as doubts about her possible pregnancy continue to torment her the latter element is elaborated by the use of nouns and adjectives which suggest a progressive decrease in brightness (*fulgor, encendida luminaria, fanal radiosísimo, lámpara, candil, chispa microscópica*), paralleling her decline.

The complexity of Díaz Rodríguez' imagery, however, depends even more heavily on two other characteristics, which are interrelated to a considerable degree: (1) the factualness of the comparison, and (2) the degree of directness of the association between the elements comprising the image.

In an image such as *zafiro del mar* (*Sangre* 70), for example, the basis for comparison is an attribute which is, according to the usual understanding of the meaning of the terms involved, actually possessed by the two elements of the image--the color blue. The analogy is thus a factual one; that is, based on empirical reality. This is not to say that psychologically the comparison may not evoke other associated impressions as well. To some readers the image might convey an impression of depth, or of light, or of some other notion, as well as that of blueness. It is only to say that the essential basis for the comparison is factual.

This factual type of image is common in all of the novels. However, a type of image that is not factual also occurs. It appears to some extent in *Idolos* and in *Peregrina*; in *Sangre* it is more frequent than the factual type, and perhaps more than any other single element serves to mark the style of this novel as quintessentially modernistic.

One of the relatively few non-factual images in *Idolos* describes a sunset: "el crepúsculo se desmayaba, por fin, desangrándose por sus enormes heridas purpúreas, en los brazos de la noche" (358). As is apparent, the image involves some extension. There are three comparisons, all of which are intimately related to the total image. Dusk is compared with the act of excessive bleeding, the coming of dusk is likened to the act of swooning, and night is given the property of having arms. In none of the comparisons is the analogy based on empirical fact, although all of them are very provocative notions. What is involved is a shift in the manner in which language is employed as a basis for analogy from that which is primarily factual to that which might be called purely evocative. To put it another way, the terms employed here are being used not to describe phenomena which are real, but rather to evoke notions by means of some sort of psychological association.

In the non-factual, evocative type of image there are also differences in the relative degree of directness of the associations involved, and these differences follow the same pattern in the novels as does the occurrence of factual and non-factual comparisons: in *Idolos* and *Peregrina* the associations are virtually always direct or only somewhat indirect, whereas in *Sangre* they are frequently quite indirect.

In the following analyses, an association of elements in an analogy is said to be direct when there would be a high degree of consensus on the essential nature of the association, although other notions besides this essential basis might be suggested as well. This implies that there would be a fairly limited range of possibilities of interpretation of the analogy. An association is said to be more indirect proportionately as the range of possibilities of interpretation of the analogy widens and as the probability of consensus on the essential nature of the association decreases. Obviously, the degree of wideness of range of interpretation of an analogy may depend on various factors. The association may, at one extreme, be quite apparent and require no special knowledge to interpret. It may, on the other hand, be based on some special use of a term, such as the modernists' symbolic use of words like *cisne* or *azul*, or it may be linked to a wider context in the work in which it appears. The interpretation of such an association would depend on some kind of special knowledge, and in many cases it would imply a wider range of possibilities of interpretation. At the other extreme, the association may be, theoretically at least, completely open-ended as to interpretation.

In the analogy of dusk and excessive bleeding in the image from *Idolos* cited above the association between the elements is fairly direct. The association of the notion of dissipation of color, specifically of red color, with both phenomena is apparent, and there would probably be a high degree of consensus that this was the essential basis for the analogy, although other notions might also be suggested, depending in part on the context in which the image occurs. It is not difficult to associate the notion of swooning or fainting with fading, as the color is doing. The analogy of arms and night is also fairly direct, since the notion associated by most readers with both terms would probably be that of enveloping, although again other notions might also be suggested.

In another non-factual, evocative image Alberto extols to his brother the beauty of a book brought from Paris: "Y con toda su belleza, en la belleza de la mano, sería como una gota de agua con todos los esplendores del Azul posada sobre un pétalo" (198). Here the associations are less direct, and the interpretation depends in part on the special use of *Azul*. The basis of comparison between the book and a drop of water is that they are both said to resting on something--the book in a hand, and the drop of water on a petal--and to this extent the comparison may be said to be factual. Beyond this, books and drops of water actually have very little in common, although most readers would probably agree that the notion of beauty, associated explicitly with both book and hand, easily extends to the drop of water, especially in the context of a petal. The attribution of "todos los esplendores del Azul" to the drop of water may also be interpreted factually, since the blue of the sky may certainly be reflected in water (although perhaps with difficulty in so small an amount), and most readers would probably consider this to be beautiful as well. The fact that *Azul* is capitalized, however, suggests very strongly that it is being used in its symbolic sense, which not only strengthens the notion of beauty but inevitably suggests, to those familiar with the usage, the wider range of concepts associated by the modernists with *Azul*--love, the ideal, and the infinite.

In a few non-factual, evocative images in *Peregrina* some indirectness of association is to be noted. As Peregrina contemplates the possibility of her conceiving a child, the thought of the shame it would bring begins to obsess her: "Por la noche lo hallaba tendido en su almohada como un zarzal ardiente . . . " (156). Here the thought is said to be stretched out on her pillow, a non-factual association, which most readers would no doubt, however, take to mean that it assaulted her at night, even without the additional context which does bear out this interpretation. The comparison of the obsessive thought to a burning brier patch is quite suggestive, but not very indirect. While briers do not normally burn, intransitively, their thorns do cause pain, with which the notion of a burning sensation is easily associated. The notion that Peregrina is suffering intense psychological pain is thus reinforced by this evocation of physical pain.

Another provocative image refers to the change that occurs in Bruno following his brief encounter with the mysterious naked woman on his way to Caracas one morning. As a result of it ". . . a su imaginación comenzaban a salirle alas de ímpetu aguileño . . . " (165). The interpretation of this image does depend on the context of the following few lines, which indicate that the amorous adventure has had the effect of freeing him psychologically from everything that has tied him to the responsible, respectable, predictable type of life he would lead if he married Peregrina, and of allowing the "true Bruno" to emerge. Within this context an image in which his imagination sprouts wings that have the energy (impetus) of those of an eagle must probably be interpreted to mean that in his new-found sense of freedom his imagination suggests to him endless possible experiences.

Still another very suggestive image describes a sunset: "Gladiolas dispersas entre los rosales, erigen sus vástagos floridos, como lanzas enhiestas bajo el crepúsculo. En las puntas de algunas de esas lanzas brilla el oro y en las puntas de otras la sangre, como si fuese al golpe de ellas que el crepúsculo dorado y sangriento entró en agonía" (98). The basis for the comparison between the gladiola and lances is of course their shape, and this association is very direct. The notion of the gold and red flowers piercing the sky to cause the gold-red color of the sunset is less direct, but is facilitated by the use of *sangre* instead of *rojo*, since when lances pierce flesh they cause blood to appear, and blood also remains on the point of the lance. It is not, then, too difficult to imagine a parallel gold-tipped lance, which has acquired its color by piercing something containing gold "blood," causing that color to appear. There would no doubt be a high degree of consensus that the *agonía* of dusk refers to the final moments before its end, or death.

Díaz Rodríguez quite often describes sunsets in figurative terms, and perhaps a description of one in *Sangre* may serve as an introductory illustration of the more complex type of image characteristic of that novel. The image occurs in the description of the seascape that concludes the section in which Tulio learns of Belén's death. The sea is seen, indifferent as always, under "el cárdeno suplicio del crepúsculo" (26).

The basis for the association between *cárdeno* and *suplicio* is fairly direct, if *suplicio* is interpreted to mean "suffering" or "torment," since the purplish color implied by "livid" can be quite easily associated with bruises, and thence with some kind of suffering. The psychological connection between *suplicio* and *crepúsculo*, however, is not so clear. It may be said to be based essentially on the color, a purplish hue, common both to some kinds of suffering (principally those caused by contusions, it is presumed), and to dusk. On the other hand, the association may be taken to be based essentially on the notion of grief or sadness, which may be associated with both dusk, via the notion of the dying of day, and suffering on the part of someone. This last possibility is the association most consistent with the wider context of the novel, since it is clear that Tulio is experiencing intense grief. The notion of the protagonist's grief thus seems to be further intensified by the notion of the sadness which may be occasioned by the coming of dusk, particularly since this too is caused by a "death" (of day).

The point to be made from the above is that in this last analogy the essential basis for comparison is not as clear cut as are those of the notions of dissipation of redness in the analogy of dusk and excessive bleeding or of enveloping in the analogy of night and arms, in the sunset image cited from *Idolos*, nor the notions of pointed shape in the comparison between gladiola and lances, the notion of piercing and thus causing the appearance of red and gold in the same analogy, or that of the final moments of life in the analogy of death agony and dusk in the sunset image in *Peregrina*.

It is difficult to pinpoint the nature of the difference between two analogies one of which is perceived as being more indirect than the other. It has been stated above that the more indirect an analogy is the more open it is to a range of possible interpretations. One also senses that more imagination may be required to grasp and articulate the relationship between elements of the more indirect analogy. A third factor, however, may provide a more objective measure for the degree of directness of an analogy, and this is that there appears to be a correlation between the directness of an analogy and the relative degree of succinctness with which it can be restated in non-metaphoric language. Restatements in non-metaphoric language of the three sunset images cited above should illustrate what is entailed in this approach.

In the image from *Idolos* the reddish color of the sky usually present at sunset is fading, or dissipating, and night is enveloping or obscuring the light of day and the objects revealed by light, as arms may envelop and obscure objects. In the image from *Peregrina* stalks of gladiola are compared to lances because both are pointed in shape. Via the notion of lances causing blood to appear, the red and gold flowers seem to have caused the same colors to appear in the sky, heralding the final moments of dusk.

If, on the other hand, the image cited from *Sangre* were to be similarly restated the explanation might be something like this: The protagonist has just learned of the death of his wife, and this causes him to experience extreme sadness, grief, or suffering. The coming of dusk, which may be viewed as a death (of day), may also produce a feeling of sadness or grief. The parallel between these two grief-producing agents tends to intensify the notion of grief being experienced by the protagonist, since the death of day must remind him more forcibly of the cause of his own grief, the death of his wife. The color livid, here employed as an attribute of suffering, is in fact associated with certain kinds of suffering, principally those caused by bruises. It may, therefore, be construed as an intensifier of the notion of the suffering being experienced by the protagonist. There is also some further association to be made by the linking of the purplish hue common to some kinds of suffering to the hue which is frequently present at the coming of dusk. The association of the color livid with both the element of dusk and that of suffering intensifies further the notion of a causative connection between these two elements.[1] It must be remembered that there is always some possibility of lack of consensus on the interpretation of an image. However, a considerably greater amount of circumlocution is evidently required to articulate the (possible) essential bases of association in the analogies of the third image, revolving in this particular case largely, although not wholly, around the knowledge of a broader context in the work itself.

The degree of indirectness of association between the elements of many of the images in *Sangre* is quite striking. One of the best examples of this is the following passage, which occurs in the densely metaphoric passage describing Martí's composition: "Sobre el silencio de las aguas del río una canción pasó entonces deshojándose, como la flor misma del silencio" (65). There are three interrelated comparisons: the movement of a song over the water is likened to that of stripping, or dropping of leaves or petals, silence is said to possess some kind of flower or blossom, and these two analogies are compared in a simile.

The association between *canción* and *deshojándose* is only somewhat indirect, and can be articulated fairly succinctly in non-metaphoric language, since it must probably be taken to be a poetic manner of expressing the notion that the notes of the song are perceived as being separated, or released, from the whole, as petals may be from a flower. The occurrence of the word *flor* in the second analogy facilitates this association. The connection between *flor* and *silencio* is more indirect. The notion that a flower blooms, literally, as silence may be said, figuratively, to "bloom" may be taken to be the basis for the comparison, and the rendering would simply be, albeit in language which is not strictly non-metaphoric, the "blooming of silence." A similar interpretation might be based on the notion of blooming but include its further connotation of "the time of highest vigor, freshness and beauty," in which case *la flor misma del silencio* might be taken to suggest "the very essence of silence." On the other hand, *flor* may be taken to convey the notion of beauty, and if this were the basis for the association the rendering might be "the beauty which silence itself possesses--an ultimate sort of beauty." Depending on the interpretation given the second element, the simile which likens *canción* to *la flor misma del silencio* may be based on the most indirect association of all. If *la flor misma del silencio* is taken to convey the notion, suggested above, of "the beauty which silence itself possesses," then the simile would involve the comparison of song to beauty. It could then be said that the analogy was a factual one, since songs are in fact said to be beautiful, as silence may also be said to be. If, on the other hand, *la flor misma del silencio* is taken to mean "the blooming of silence," in the sense of "the very essence of silence," then the comparison would be between song and silence, and the interpretation would involve not only a factual contradiction but a logical one as well. The very suggestive notion of a silent song can probably be more easily imagined than something like a square circle, but it will require some circumlocution to articulate the notion in non-metaphoric language.

A restatement in non-metaphoric language of the entire image, in which the first analogy is designated A, the second B, and the third, or the simile, C, if the simile is taken to compare song to silence, might be something like this: A. The song is releasing its separate notes over the silent waters of the river, as a flower might release its petals. B. The effect of this on the hearer is that of the intense of beauty of the sound of the song, particularly as it is contrasted with the surrounding silence. Silence is also beautiful, although perhaps its beauty can best be appreciated when it is contrasted, as it is here, with its opposite, sound. In the passage song and silence are both perceived more or less simultaneously, or with very short intervals separating the occurrences of each, and so the effect of the beauty of both is perhaps intensified. The song, in effect, seems to possess the beauty that silence itself possesses. C. The song fades away, and thus becomes inaudible or "silent," but it leaves in the memories of the hearers a residue of its beauty, and this is perhaps further strengthened by the still-existing beauty of the silence which surrounds them. In this sense, perhaps, a song may be said to be "silent." It is no longer audible, but it still exists in the memories of those who heard it.

Another very striking non-factual, evocative image occurs in the passage that relates Tulio's horrified reaction to the delivery to his Paris apartment of flowers that had been intended to welcome the now dead Belén. He perceives in them a tremendous irony, "como debe ser la ironía de un dios, muda y perfumada" (32). Here there are three interrelated comparisons: *ironía de un dios*, *ironía muda*, and *ironía perfumada*.

In two of the analogies the psychological association is fairly direct. Gods are imagined to be supernatural beings and therefore any irony associated with the notion of a god must be somehow supernatural also, or of more significance than ordinary irony. Given the notion of gods, this essential association can be succinctly articulated. The association of muteness with irony is also a fairly direct one, easily articulated in non-metaphoric language. Both involve the notion of tacitness, meaning both "making no sound" (mute), and "not expressed but only implied"--irony is implied in situations or statements which have a peculiar disposition; namely, that what really is the outcome of a situation or the meaning of a statement is not what was expected. The notion of perfumed irony, however, involves an association which is much more indirect, and which requires more circumlocution to restate in non-metaphoric language. In fact, some knowledge of the context of the passage in which the image occurs is needed in order to grasp and articulate the connection. Tulio's intent, in ordering that their arrival coincide with that of the newlyweds, was that the flowers be "prevenidas . . . a deshacerse, a los pies de la novia, en epitalamios de perfume" (32). In fact, however, they now may not even serve to cover her grave, since she has none but the sea. Thus the flowers, with which the notion of perfume is readily associated, are the irony, a perfumed irony, since the situation they were intended to enhance has been so radically changed.

Perhaps one final analysis of this commonly occurring type of image will serve to clarify the importance of its role in the style of *Sangre*. As he returns to Venezuela, and his *sueño idílico* comes more and more to predominate over his *sueño épico*, Tulio begins to wish that the crossing would never end, as do those who engage in shipboard romances: "todos aquellos cuyo idilio floreció como una rosa de aire azul entre las jarcias" (81).

Here again there are three interrelated comparisons. An idyll, in context understood to mean "idyllic love affair," is said to flower or bloom, a rose is said to be of blue air, and these two analogies are compared in a simile. Two of the analogies may be said to be based on fact, as both the love affair and the rose are linked to the verb *florecer*, which comprehends the meaning of "to flourish" as well as "to blossom." A love affair may, in ordinary parlance, be said to flourish (metaphorically to blossom) as a rose may be said to blossom. The analogy *rosa de aire azul*, however, is clearly not factual. Moreover, the psychological association between the terms "rose" and "blue air" is quite indirect; some special knowledge is required in this case to grasp the connection, and some degree of circumlocution necessary to articulate it in non-metaphoric language.

It will be recalled that the modernists frequently employed the color blue symbolically to suggest notions such as beauty, love, the ideal, or the infinite. The sky, of course, is blue, and must have served as a constant reminder of the connection which they made between the infinite and the color blue, or perhaps have been the origin of the connection. A rose made of the same stuff as the sky, then, might be said to be an infinite, ideal, sort of rose, and the nature of a love affair might well in this case be analogous to such a rose.[2]

Non-factual, evocative images based on indirect associations may be said to be predominantly symbolistic in technique, since the terms involved in the analogies are employed not on the basis of their meanings so much as upon their suggestiveness. Furthermore, it would seem to follow that proportionately as an analogy is more open to various interpretations, or the more indirect the psychological association between the elements, the more typically symbolistic the analogy may be said to be.

It should perhaps be recalled here that one of the principal characteristics of the post-modernist writers was that they frequently associated terms together on a purely emotive rather than on a primarily factual basis, and that this was, furthermore, an essential element in the evolution of the style of these writers from that of the modernists. The fact that Díaz Rodríguez' use of this technique, initiated somewhat hesitantly in *Idolos*, reaches a peak in *Sangre* marks him at that point as not only the consummate modernist novelist but as a precursor of subsequent literary movements. In spite of the *criollista* orientation of *Peregrina*, one cannot but be somewhat surprised at the stylistic about-face represented by the great diminution in the use of this particular device in that novel, and one wonders whether he would have returned to the technique had he lived to continue his literary production.

Imagery, which is often although by no means always based on sense impressions, is very common in the three novels. The density of imagery is much higher in *Sangre* than in the other two works, especially *Peregrina*, in which true density is rare. The occurrence of non-factual, evocative images is also much more common in *Sangre*; these occur infrequently in *Idolos* and even less frequently in *Peregrina*. In the non-factual, evocative type of image the association between elements is quite often considerably more indirect in those of *Sangre* than in those of the other two novels, and the symbolistic nature of these images marks the Díaz Rodríguez of *Sangre* as a precursor of post-modernism, a position he can no longer be said to occupy at the writing of *Peregrina*.

NOTES

[1] The multiple meanings of *suplicio* complicate the interpretation of the image. For purposes of analysis I have taken it to mean "suffering." The attribution to it of another meaning--"execution," for example--would not alter the point being made here.

[2] As Cirlot points out, the blue rose traditionally symbolizes the impossible (275), which is also appropriate in this context, but the additional link with *aire* demands a modernistic interpretation.

CONCLUSIONS

The artistry of Díaz Rodríguez' style is to be noted not only in its virtuosity but also in its adaptation to the natures of his three quite dissimilar novels. While there are many constants--the attention to sense impressions, especially color, the use of "favorite" words, the manipulation of syntactic periods, and the use of figurative language, for example--there are striking differences between the novels, revealing a style that is not only virtuosic but exceedingly dynamic.

Rarely is a specific device used in the same way in all three works, or even in any two of them. There are a few exceptions, such as the symbolic use of auditory sensations and the association of these with structure, which are very similar in *Idolos* and *Sangre*. In the application of nearly all of the other devices some adaptation is noted.

Most of the adaptations are explained by the nature of the works themselves. There is, for example, a clear pattern of evolution/devolution in the use of some devices as Díaz Rodríguez moves from the early modernism of *Idolos* to the quintessential modernism of *Sangre* and then to the more realistic, if idealized, *criollismo* of *Peregrina*. This pattern is noted in 1) the use of figurative language to evoke sense impressions, 2) the figurative use of the "favorite" words *alma, ensueño/sueño*, and *idílico/idilio*, 3) the symbolic function of color, 4) the symbolic use of the "favorite" words *belleza/bello* and *ensueño/sueño*, and the linking of these to elements of plot or structure, 5) the use of syntactic motifs, and 6) the density and complexity of the imagery, all of which increase in frequency and effectiveness from *Idolos* to *Sangre* and either decrease (1, 2, 5, 6) or disappear (3, 4) in *Peregrina*.

Its *criollista* focus also explains three other differences in the application of devices in *Peregrina*: the non-symbolic use color, the increased frequency and range of auditory sensations, and the evocation of actual taste sensations.

The overall use of color and auditory sensations must be said to be most artistically effective in *Idolos* and *Sangre*, in which they are sometimes used symbolically and integrated into structural elements. In *Peregrina*, in which evocations of color and sound are usually employed in descriptions of aspects of the natural setting, appropriate adaptations have been made. As Dunham points out, nature may be said to assume the role of protagonist in *Peregrina*, so predominant is its presence (38), and this emphasis is a clear indication of Díaz Rodríguez' profound love of the Avila and the countryside surrounding it, the setting of *Peregrina* (77). That a stylist of Díaz Rodríguez' virtuosity should choose to introduce new color words, to place increased emphasis on subtle shadings, to maintain the tendency to evoke a wide range of colors, and to increase the frequency and range of auditory sensations in a novel in which nature

85

plays such a predominant role is not surprising. The fact that actual taste sensations,although not frequent, are more common in *Peregrina* than in either of the other novels is also appropriate to its *criollista* focus.

There are a number of other differences in the use of stylistic devices between the novels which relate not so much to the nature of the works as to wider contexts within them.

Red is the color most often used symbolically in *Idolos*; white is sometimes juxtaposed with red in this function, and blue is occasionally symbolic. Although these same colors, together with green and black, occur symbolically in *Sangre*, none of them predominates in the same way; instead, they are interrelated in a rather complex manner. This difference in emphasis is quite in keeping with the wider context of the novels. One might expect red symbolism to predominate in *Idolos*, with its highly charged but relatively straightforward emphasis on physical passion and war, whereas the more intricate structure of *Sangre* would seem to demand the more complex use of color symbolism that does in fact occur.

Imaginary sounds are voices in *Idolos* and *Sangre*, and are linked to the psychological states of the protagonists, one a typically modernist maladjusted artist, and the other a typical modernist *abuliac* (also maladjusted), both aristocrats at odds with reality. That these high-strung individuals should hear voices, which are in both cases hostile and threatening, is not inappropriate. On the other hand, it is difficult to imagine any of the simple folk of *Peregrina* hearing such a voice. It is, however, appropriate and believable that the imaginary sound in that novel--the strange music issuing from the *pozo encantado*--be linked to folk belief.

Although unpleasant odors are not frequently evoked in *Idolos*, their occasional presence is appropriate to the much more negative, even bitter, tone of that novel as compared to the others. The virtual absence of unpleasant odors in *Sangre* comes as no surprise, of course, although it is somewhat surprising that there are none in *Peregrina*. That this should be the case must be attributed to the author's tendency to idealize in *Peregrina*, in spite of the novel's *criollista* emphasis. The proportionately much higher frequency of *amargo/amargura* in a non-actual sense in *Idolos* also reflects the bitterness of the author's criticism of the socio-political situation in Venezuela, which is much more apparent here than in *Sangre*, and which is avoided in *Peregrina*.

The different treatment of extended emphasis on tactile sensations in *Idolos* and *Sangre* is also tied to context. In *Sangre* the passages, which describe the sensation of water on his flesh as Tulio descends into the dream world, have clearly sensual overtones, but there is no clear association with the erotic. On the other hand, in the passages describing the sensation of water on Teresa Farías' flesh as she bathes in the sea and imagines it to be a giant, formless lover, the association is quite clearly erotic. This difference responds to the wider context of the sexuality of the two characters--there is no emphasis on this aspect of

86

Tulio's personality, but we know from the outset that Teresa is an extremely sexual woman. The different approach to the stylistic device is also appropriate to the wider context of the nature of the relationship between Tulio and Belén, which is essentially chaste, and the overtly sexual relationship between Alberto and Teresa. The evocation of odors associated with the sexual act, noted only in *Idolos*, also responds to this context.

The continued, even increased, use of "branching" sentences in *Peregrina* cannot be attributed to the *criollista* nature of the novel, nor to the wider context surrounding any instance of the device. Although it may be due simply to Díaz Rodríguez' fondness for the device, there is another possible explanation. At the writing of *Peregrina* Díaz Rodríguez had been active in politics for some years and was frequently called upon to deliver public addresses. "Branching" sentences, the rhythmic effect of which is especially noticeable when they are read aloud, occur with some frequency in these addresses. Although the device is frequently used in both the earlier novels as well (revealing, perhaps, a natural talent for oratory), his increased activity as an orator at the time of the writing of *Peregrina* may well have been a factor in the prevalence of the technique in his last novel. Whatever the reason for its retention, the use of the device in *Peregrina* is one of the most significant features marking the continuity of modernistic techniques in the three works.

Also significant in this continuity is the use of imagery. Although both the density and the complexity of imagery follow the evolution/devolution pattern, increasing from *Idolos* to *Sangre* and decreasing in *Peregrina*, it is revealing to note in *Peregrina* the occurrence of some very vivid and imaginative metaphors. Clearly, the use of metaphor is another area in which Díaz Rodríguez the modernist is still effective at the writing of *Peregrina*.

As Díaz Rodríguez' style evolves in his three novels, it follows a trajectory that responds in part to his increasing involvement with modernistic techniques and then to a blending of some of these with *criollista* elements. The numerous variations in the specific use of devices that complement this pattern attest not only to his continued attachment to the Modernist mode but to his masterful ability to adapt favored techniques to the quite dissimilar natures of the novels. Although in the areas of metaphor, symbolism, and the manipulation of syntactic periods *Sangre* emerges as the example *par excellence* of the novelist's artistry, this artistry is also quite evident in the other two novels, whether it be in the nascent form of some techniques noted in *Idolos*, the attenuated treatment of some noted in *Peregrina*, or in effective adaptations of techniques to the novels themselves. In all three works Díaz Rodríguez justifies his well-deserved reputation as the most accomplished literary stylist of his generation.

TABLE I

Numerical Frequency of Occurrence (Total)	Page Percentage Frequency of Occurrence (100 x Total Occurrence ÷ No. of Pages)		
	Idolos	*Sangre*	*Peregrina*
	(206 pp.)	(90 pp.)	(101 pp.)
1	0.48%	1.11%	0.99%
2	0.97	2.22	1.98
3	1.45	3.33	2.97
4	1.94	4.44	3.96
5	2.42	5.55	4.95
6	2.91	6.66	5.94
7	3.39	7.77	6.93
8	3.88	8.88	7.92
9	4.36	10.00	8.91
10	4.85	11.11	9.90
20	9.70	22.22	19.80
30	14.56	33.33	29.70
40	19.41	44.44	39.60
50	24.27	55.55	49.50
60	29.12	66.66	
70	33.98	77.77	
80	38.83		
90	43.68		
96	46.60	95.04	
100	48.54		
109			107.92
113	54.85		
128	62.13		
135			150.00
168			186.66
180	87.38		
200	96.98		
221			245.55
293	142.23		
382	185.43		

TABLE II

Frequency of Occurrence of Color Words

	Idolos	*Sangre*	*Peregrina*
Total Color Words	**142.23%**	**246.66%**	**204.95%**
Generic Red	**43.20%**	**54.44%**	**52.47%**
bermejo	0	1.11	1.98
cárdeno	0	1.11	0
carmesí	0.48	0	0
carmín	0	1.11	0
flamígero	0	0	0.99
fuego	3.39	0	2.97
granate	0	0	0.99
inflamado	0.97	0	0
inflamar	0.97	0	0.99
llama	1.45	1.11	1.98
llamarada	1.94	0	0.99
empurpurar	0	1.11	0.99
purpúreo	5.33	3.33	1.98
púrpuro	6.79	10.00	9.90
rojeante	0	0	0.99
rojez	0	0	0.99
rojizo	0	0	0.99
rojo	7.28	6.66	9.90
rosa	5.82	8.88	4.95
rosado	1.94	1.11	0
rosal	0.48	1.11	0
róseo	0	3.33	0
sonrosado	0.48	0	0
rubí	1.94	0	0.99
rubor	2.42	1.11	0.99
desangrar	0.48	0	0
ensangrentar	0	1.11	0.99
sangre	0.97	11.11	5.94
sangriente	0	1.11	1.98

89

	Idolos	*Sangre*	*Peregrina*
Generic White	**32.52%**	**53.33%**	**38.61%**
albo	1.45	1.11	0.99
albor	0.48	0	0
albura	0.48	1.11	0
armiño	0	1.11	0
blanco	18.44	26.66	22.77
blancor	0.48	0	0
blancura	3.39	3.33	3.96
blanquear	0.48	1.11	0.99
blanquísimo	0.97	0	0
blanquito	0	0	1.98
candidez	0.97	3.33	0
candidísimo	0	0	0.99
cándido	2.42	14.44	3.96
nieve	2.91	1.11	2.97
Generic Green	**11.16%**	**56.66%**	**22.77%**
esmeralda	0.97	5.55	1.98
glauco	1.45	18.88	0.99
turquesa	0	1.11	0
verde	6.31	24.44	14.85
verdeante	0.48	1.11	0
verdear	0.48	0	0
verdeobscuro	0	0	0.99
verdinegro	0	0	0.99
verdor	0.48	2.22	0.99
verdoso	0	0	0.99
verdura	0.97	3.33	0.99
Generic Blue	**17.47%**	**51.11%**	**8.91%**
azul	16.50	44.44	8.91
celeste	0.48	1.11	0
cerúleo	0.48	0	0.00
zafiro	0	5.55	0

	Idolos	*Sangre*	*Peregrina*
Generic Yellow	**20.87%**	**18.88%**	**39.60%**
amarilleado	0	0	0.99
amarillento	0.48	0	0
amarillez	0.48	0	0.99
amarillito	0	0	1.98
amarillo	2.42	0	5.94
ámbar	0	0	2.97
áureo	3.39	5.55	3.96
dorado	0.48	2.22	1.98
gualdo	1.45	0	0
ocre	1.94	0	1.98
oro	6.31	10.00	16.83
rubio	3.88	1.11	1.98
Generic Black	**12.13%**	**10.00%**	**14.85%**
azabache	0	0	0.99
ébano	0	0	0.99
negrear	0	0	1.98
negrísimo	0.48	0	0
negro	11.16	10.00	9.90
negruzco	0.48	0	0.99
Generic Purple	**1.45%**	**0%**	**10.89%**
amatista	0	0	1.98
lila	0.48	0	1.98
malvo	0.48	0	0.99
morado	0	0	1.98
violeta	0.48	0	3.96
Generic Gray	**2.42%**	**2.22%**	**5.94%**
acero	0	1.11	0
gris	1.94	1.11	4.95
plomizo	0.48	0	0.99

	Idolos	*Sangre*	*Peregrina*
Generic Brown	**0.48%**	**0%**	**4.95%**
cobrizo	0	0	2.97
pardo	0.48	0	0.99
pardoamarillento	0	0	0.99
Generic Silver	**0.48%**	**0%**	**4.95%**
plata	0.48	0	4.95
Generic Orange	**0%**	**0%**	**0.99%**
anaranjado	0	0	0.99

TABLE III

Frequency of Occurrence of Olfactory Words

	Idolos	*Sangre*	*Peregrina*
Total Olfactory Words	**29.61%**	**41.11%**	**18.81%**
aroma	1.94	4.44	2.97
esencia	2.91	1.11	0
fragancia/fragante	9.22	15.55	4.95
incienso	1.45	0	1.98
oliente/olor/oloroso	2.91	5.55	3.96
perfumado/perfumar/perfume	11.16	14.44	4.95

Frequency of Occurrence of Tactile Words Referring to

Actual Tactile Sensations

	Idolos	*Sangre*	*Peregrina*
Total Actual Tactile Words	**38.83%**	**23.33%**	**17.82%**
aspereza/áspero	0.97	2.22	2.97
besar/beso	16.01	11.11	6.93
acariciar/caricia	15.53	8.88	3.96
raso	0.48	0	0.99
seda/sedeño/sedoso	1.94	0	0.99
suave/suavidad/suavísimo/			
suavizado	2.91	1.11	0.99
terciopelo	0.97	0	0.99

Frequency of Occurrence of Tactile Words Referring to

Non-Actual Tactile Sensations

	Idolos	*Sangre*	*Peregrina*
Total Non-Actual Tactile Words	**23.30%**	**50.00%**	**20.79%**
aspereza/áspero	5.33	4.44	2.97
besar/beso	3.39	12.11	0
acariciar/caricia	4.85	4.44	0.99
raso	0.48	2.22	0
seda/sedante/sedeño	2.42	5.55	2.97
suave/suavemente/suavidad/			
suavísimo/suavizar	6.79	21.11	13.86

TABLE Va

Frequency of Occurrence of Taste Words Referring to

Actual Taste Sensations

	Idolos	*Sangre*	*Peregrina*
Total Actual Taste Words	**0%**	**8.88%**	**9.90%**
ácido	0	0	1.98
amargo/amargura	0	2.22	0.99
áspero	0	0	2.97
dulce	0	0	1.98
sabor/saborear/sabrosísimo/sabroso	0	4.44	1.98
salsedumbre	0	2.22	0

TABLE Vb

Frequency of Occurrence of Taste Words Referring to

Non-Actual Taste Sensations

	Idolos	*Sangre*	*Peregrina*
Total Non-Actual Taste Words	**38.83%**	**38.88%**	**25.74%**
acerbidad/acerbo	2.91	2.22	0.99
ácido	0.97	1.11	0
amargar/amargo/amargura	8.25	2.22	0
aspereza/áspero	0.97	0	0
dulce/dulcificar/dulzón/dulzura	14.07	27.77	20.79
sabor/saborear/sabrosísimo/sabroso	11.65	4.44	3.96
sal	0	1.11	0

94

TABLE VI

Frequency of Occurrence of "Favorite Words"

	Idolos	*Sangre*	*Peregrina*
Total Favorite Words	**185.43%**	**186.66%**	**45.54%**
alma	87.38	75.55	19.80
belleza/bello/bellamente/ bellísimo/embellecer/ embellecido	54.85	47.77	11.88
diafanidad/diáfano	1.94	11.11	3.96
idílico/idilio	2.91	15.55	1.98
ensueño/sueño	16.99	30.00	3.96
voluptuosidad/voluptuoso	21.35	6.66	3.96

WORKS CITED

Agudo Freytes, Raúl. "El anacronismo literario de Díaz Rodríguez." *Revista Nacional de Cultura* 67 (1948): 147-56.

Alonso, Dámaso, and Carlos Bousoño. *Seis calas en la expresión literaria española.* 2nd ed. Madrid: Gredos, 1956.

Anderson Imbert, Enrique. *Historia de la literatura hispanoamericana.* México: Fondo de Cultura Económica, 1954.

Angarita Arvelo, Rafael. *Historia y crítica de la novela en Venezuela.* Berlin: Imprenta de August Pries, Leipzig, 1938.

Araujo, Orlando. *La palabra estéril.* Maracaibo: Universidad de Zulia, Facultad de Humanidades y Educación, 1966.

Benítez, Jorge. "Hacia el surrealismo de *Sangre patricia* de Manuel Díaz Rodríguez." *Estudios críticos sobre la prosa modernista.* Ed. José Olivio Jiménez. New York: Eliseo Torres and Sons, 1975. 255-68.

Castro, José Antonio. "La disolución del mundo exterior en *Sangre patricia.*" Revista *de Literatura Hispanoamericana* 4 (1973): 53-69.

Cirlot, J. E. *A Dictionary of Symbols.* 2nd ed. New York: Philosophical Library, 1971.

Crema, Edoardo. "Armonía de tendencias en *Peregrina.*" *Revista Nacional de Cultura* 136 (1959): 89-106.

Debicki, Andrew P. "Manuel Díaz Rodríguez's *Sangre patricia*: A Point of View Novel." *Hispania* 53 (1970): 59-66.

Díaz Rodríguez, Manuel. *Camino de perfección.* Paris: Sociedad de Ediciones Literarias y Artísticas,

n. d..

---. *Idolos rotos.* Caracas: Colección Clásicos Venezolanos de la Academia Venezolana de la Lengua, tomo I, 1964.

---. *Peregrina o el pozo encantado*. Caracas: Colección Clásicos Venezolanos de la Academia Venezolana de la Lengua, tomo II, 1964.

---. *Sangre patricia*. Caracas: Coleccion Clasicos Venezolanos de la Academia Venezolana de la Lengua, tomo II, 1964.

Díaz Seijas, Pedro. *La antigua y la moderna literatura venezolana*. Caracas: Editorial Armitano, 1966.

Di Prisco, Rafael. *Acerca de los orígenes de la novela venezolana*. Caracas: Universidad Central de Caracas, Dirección de Cultura, 1969.

Dunham, Lowell. *Manuel Díaz Rodríguez: Vida y Obra*. México: Ediciones de Andrea, 1959.

Fraser, Howard M. "El universo psicodélico de *Sangre patricia*." *Hispanófila* 50 (1974): 9-18.

Goić, Cedomil. *Historia de la literatura hispanoamericana*. Valparaíso: Editorial Universidad de Valparaíso, 1972.

Holdsworth, Carole, A. "Some Modernist 'Manías Verbales' and their Connotations, in the 'Revista Moderna.'" *Hispania* 55 (1972): 60-65.

Latcham, Ricardo A. "El modernismo esteticista de Manuel Díaz Rodríguez." *Carnet crítico*. Montevideo: Editorial Alfa, 1962. 23-29.

Matteson, Marianna M. "Motivos sintácticos en *Sangre patricia*." *Explicación de Textos Literarios* II. 2 (1974): 131-36.

Matteson, Marianna Merritt. "The Symbolic Use of Color in Díaz Rodríguez' *Sangre patricia*." *Hispania* 68 (1985): 35-43.

---. "Syntactic Patterns in Díaz Rodriguez' *Idolos rotos*." *Selecta* 5 (1984): 116-21.

Olivares, Jorge. "Disposición, argumento invisible y estructura de *Sangre patricia*." *Hispanic Review* 50. 1 (1982): 17-31.

---. *La novela decadente en Venezuela*. Caracas: Gráficas Armitano, C. A., 1984.

Persaud, Loknath. "A Re-evaluation of Manuel Díaz Rodríguez' Fictional Works." Diss. SUNY Buffalo, 1980.

Phillips, Allen W. "El arte y el artista en algunas novelas modernistas." *Temas del modernismo hispánico y otros estudios*. Madrid: Gredos, 1974. 260-93.

Picón-Salas, Mariano. *Estudios de literatura venezolana*. Caracas-Madrid: Editorial Edime, 1961.

Ratcliff, Dillwyn F. *Venezuelan Prose Fiction*. New York: Instituto de las Españas, 1933.

Torres Rioseco, Arturo. "Manuel Díaz Rodríguez." *Grandes novelistas de la América Hispana*. Vol. 2. Berkeley and Los Angeles: University of California Press, 1943. 59-88.

Unamuno, Miguel de. "*Sangre patricia*." Rev. of *Sangre patricia* by Manuel Díaz Rodríguez. *El Cojo Ilustrado* 15 June 1903: 371-75.

Uslar-Pietri, Arturo. *Letras y hombres de Venezuela*. Caracas-Madrid: Editorial Edime, 1958.

Woods, Richard D. "*Sangre patricia* and the Doors of Perception." *Romance Notes* 12 (1971): 302-06.

ADDITIONAL BIBLIOGRAPHY

Alonso, Dámaso. *Materia y forma en poesía*. Madrid: Gredos, 1955.

Anderson, Robert Roland. "Manuel Díaz Rodríguez." *Spanish American Modernism: A Selected Bibliography*. Tucson: University of Arizona Press, 1970.

Aveledo Urbaneja, Agustín. "Panegírico de Manuel Díaz Rodríguez." *Cultura Venezolana* 82 (1927): 16-23.

Blanco, Andrés Eloy. "Elegía de la piedra." *Poda*. Caracas: Editorial Elite, 1934. 238-41.

Blanco Fombona, Rufino. *El modernismo y los poetas modernistas*. Madrid: Editorial Mundo Latino, 1929.

Bonilla, Manuel Antonio. "Manuel Díaz Rodríguez." *Boletín de la Academia Venezolana* 12 (1945): 256-61.

Buxó, José Pascual. "La perfección del amor en los cuentos de Manuel Díaz Rodríguez." *Anuario de Filología* 5.5 (1966): 183-98.

Carden, Poe. "Parnassianism, Symbolism, Decandentism--and Spanish American Modernism." *Hispania* 43 (1960): 545-51.

Carter, Boyd G. "Gutiérrez Nájera y Martí como iniciadores del modernismo." *Revista Iberoamericana* 28 (1962): 295-310.

Castro, José Antonio. *Narrativa modernista y concepción del mundo*. Maracaibo: Universidad del Zulia, Centro de Estudios Literarios, 1973.

Cornwell, Diane W. "El modernismo hispanoamericano visto por los modernistas." *Estudios críticos sobre la prosa modernista*. Ed. José Olivio Jiménez. New York: Eliseo Torres and Sons, 1975. 305-21.

Craig, George Dundas. *The Modernist Trend in Spanish American Poetry*. Berkeley: University of California Press, 1934.

Crow, John A. "Some Aspects of Literary Style." *Hispania* 38 (1955): 393-403.

Díaz Plaja, Guillermo. *Modernismo frente a noventa y ocho: una introducción a la literatura española del siglo XX*. Madrid: Espasa-Calpe, 1951.

Díaz Rodríguez, Manuel. *Confidencias de Psiquis*. Caracas: Colección Clásicos Venezolanos de la Academia Venezolana de la Lengua, tomo I, 1964.

---. *Cuentos de color*. Caracas: Colección Clásicos Venezolanos de la Academia Venezolana de la Lengua, tomo I, 1964.

---. *De mis romerías*. Caracas-Barcelona: Ediciones Nueva Cádiz, n. d.

--- . *Entre las colinas en flor*. Barcelona: Editorial Araluce, 1935.

--. *Sensaciones de viaje*. Caracas-Barcelona: Ediciones Nueva Cádiz, n.d.

---. *Sermones líricos*. Caracas-Barcelona: Ediciones Nueva Cádiz, n. d.

Flores, Angel. "Díaz Rodríguez, Manuel." *Bibliografía de escritores hispanoamericanos*. New York: Gordian Press, 1975.

García-Girón, Edmundo. "'La azul sonrisa.' Discusión de la adjetivación modernista." *Revista Iberoamericana* 20 (1955): 95-116.

Goldberg, Isaac. *Studies in Spanish American Literature*. New York: Brentano's, 1920.

Gullón, Germán. "Técnicas narrativas en la novela realista y en la modernista." *Cuadernos Hispanoamericanos* 286 (1974): 173-87.

Hazera, Lydia D. The Spanish American Modernist Novel and the Psychology of the Artistic Personality." *Hispanic Journal* 8.1 (1986): 69-83.

Henríquez Ureña, Max. *Breve historia del modernismo.* México: Fondo de Cultura Económica, 1954.

Holland, Henry. "Manuel Díaz Rodríguez, estilista del modernismo." *Hispania* 39 (1956): 281-86.

Larubia-Prado, Francisco. "*Sangre patricia*: La aventura del héroe mítico en la novela modernista." *Revista canadiense de estudios hispánicos* 13.2 (1989): 255-60.

Martínez, José Luis. "*Sangre patricia* y su énfasis en los sueños y el inconsciente: Manuel Díaz Rodríguez y Freud." *Dactylus* 10 (1990): 103-107.

Matlowsky, Bernice D. *Bibliografía del modernismo.* Washington: Unión Panamericana, 1952.

Matteson, Marianna M. "Imagery in Díaz Rodríguez' *Sangre patricia.*" *Hispania* 56 (1973): 1014-20.

Monguió, Luis. "Manuel Díaz Rodríguez y el conflicto entre lo práctico y lo ideal." *Estudios sobre literatura hispanoamericana y española.* México: Ediciones de Andrea, 1958. 71-77.

---. "Sobre la caracterización del modernismo." *Revista Iberoamericana* 7.13 (1943): 69- 80.

Núñez, Enrique B. *Ensayos biográficos.* Caracas: Editorial Elite, 1931.

Núñez de Cela, Nadine E. "Four Artist-Hero Novels of the Modernista Movement in Spanish America." Diss. University of Toronto, 1973.

Paz Castillo, Fernando. *De la época modernista (1892-1910).* Caracas: Editorial Arte, 1968.

Picón-Febres, Gonzalo. *La literatura venezolana en el siglo diez y nueve.* Caracas: Empresa El Cojo, 1906.

Rodríguez Chicharro, César. "Cuatro aspectos del modernismo." *Texto crítico* 4 (1976): 134-48.

Ruiz Barrionuevo, Carmen. "Manuel Díaz Rodríguez y la ficción modernista: A propósito de *Idolos rotos.*" In Chang-Rodríguez, Raquel and de Beer, Gabriella, eds., *La historia en la literatura iberoamericana: Textos del XXVI Congreso del Instituto Internacional de Literatura Iberoamericana.* New York: Ed. del Norte/City Univ. of New York, 1989.

Schwartz, Kessel. *A New History of Spanish-American Fiction.* Vol. 1. Coral Gables: University of Miami Press, 1972.

Shulman, Iván A. "Función y sentido del color en la poesía de Manuel Gutiérrez Nájera." *Revista Hispánica Moderna* 23 (1957): 1-13.

---. "Genesis del azul modernista." *Estudios críticos sobre el modernismo.* Ed. Homero Castillo. Madrid: Gredos, 1968. 168-89.

---. *Símbolo y color en la obra de Jose Martí.* Madrid: Gredos, 1960.

Silva Castro, Raúl. "El ciclo de 'lo azul' en Rubén Darío." *Estudios críticos sobre el modernismo.* Ed. Homero Castillo. Madrid: Gredos, 1968. 146-67.

---. "¿Es posible definir el modernismo?" *Cuadernos Americanos* 24 (1965): 172-79.

Silva Uzcátegui, R. D. *Historia crítica del modernismo en la literatura castellana.* Barcelona: Imprenta Viuda de Luis Tasso, 1925.

Skard, Sigmund. "The Use of Color in Literature." *Proceedings of the American Philosophical Society* 90.3 (1946): 163-249.

Subero, Efraín. *Contribución a la bibliografía de Manuel Díaz Rodríguez.* Caracas: Universidad Católica Andrés Bello, Seminario de Literatura Venezolana, 1967.

Toro y Gisbert, Miguel de. "El vocabulario de Manuel Díaz Rodríguez." *Los nuevos derroteros del idioma.* Paris: Roger y Chernoviz, 1918. 50-59.

Ullmann, Stephen. *Language and Style.* Oxford: Basil Blackwell, 1964.

Vidal, Hernán. "*Sangre patricia* y la conjunción naturalista-simbolista." *Hispania* 52 (1969): 183-92.

Zum Felde, Alberto. *Indice crítico de la literatura hispanoamericana. La narrativa.* Vol. 2. México: Editorial Guarania, 1959.

Scripta Humanistica

Directed by
BRUNO M. DAMIANI
The Catholic University of America
COMPREHENSIVE LIST OF PUBLICATIONS*

1. Everett W. Hesse, *The "Comedia" and Points of View.* $24.50
2. Marta Ana Diz, *Patronio y Lucanor: la lectura inteligente "en el tiempo que es turbio."* Prólogo de John Esten Keller. $26.00
3. James F. Jones, Jr., *The Story of a Fair Greek of Yesteryear.* A Translation from the French of Antoine-François Prévost's *L'Histoire d'une Grecque moderne.* With Introduction and Selected Bibliography. $30.00
4. Colette H. Winn, *Jean de Sponde: Les sonnets de la mort ou La Poétique de l'accoutumance.* Préface par Frédéric Deloffre. $22.50
5. Jack Weiner, *"En busca de la justicia social: estudio sobre el teatro español del Siglo de Oro."* $24.50
6. Paul A. Gaeng, *Collapse and Reorganization of the Latin Nominal Flection as Reflected in Epigraphic Sources.* Written with the assistance of Jeffrey T. Chamberlin. $24.00
7. Edna Aizenberg, *The Aleph Weaver: Biblical, Kabbalistic, and Judaic Elements in Borges.* $25.00
8. Michael G. Paulson and Tamara Alvarez-Detrell, *Cervantes, Hardy, and "La fuerza de la sangre."* $25.50
9. Rouben Charles Cholakian, *Deflection/Reflection in the Lyric Poetry of Charles d'Orléans: A Psychosemiotic Reading.* $25.00
10. Kent P. Ljungquist, *The Grand and the Fair: Poe's Landscape Aesthetics and Pictorial Techniques.* $27.50
11. D.W. McPheeters, *Estudios humanísticos sobre la "Celestina."* $20.00
12. Vittorio Felaco, *The Poetry and Selected Prose of Camillo Sbarbaro.* Edited and Translated by Vittorio Felaco. With a Preface by Franco Fido. $25.00
13. María del C. Candau de Cevallos, *Historia de la lengua española.* $33.00
14. *Renaissance and Golden Age Studies in Honor of D.W. McPheeters.* Ed. Bruno M. Damiani. $30.00
15. Bernardo Antonio González, *Parábolas de identidad: Realidad interior y estrategia narrativa en tres novelistas de posguerra.* $28.00
16. Carmelo Gariano, *La Edad Media (Aproximación Alfonsina).* $30.00
17. Gabriella Ibieta, *Tradition and Renewal in "La gloria de don Ramiro".* $27.50
18. *Estudios literarios en honor de Gustavo Correa.* Eds. Charles Faulhaber, Richard Kinkade, T.A. Perry. Preface by Manuel Durán. $25.00
19. George Yost, *Pieracci and Shelly: An Italian Ur-Cenci.* $27.50

20. Zelda Irene Brooks, *The Poetry of Gabriel Celaya*. $26.00
21. *La relación o naufragios de Alvar Núñez Cabeza de Vaca*,
    eds. Martin A. Favata y José B. Fernández. $27.50
22. Pamela S. Brakhage, *The Theology of "La Lozana andalu-
    za."* $27.50
23. Jorge Checa, *Gracián y la imaginación arquitectónica*. $28.00
24. Gloria Gálvez Lira, *Maria Luisa Bombal: realidad y fantasía*. $28.50
25. Susana Hernández Araico, *Ironía y tragedia en Calderón*. $25.00
26. Philip J. Spartano, *Giacomo Zanella: Poet, Essayist, and
    Critic of the "Risorgimento."* Preface by Roberto Severino. $24.00
27. E. Kate Stewart, *Arthur Sherburne Hardy: Man of American
    Letters*. Preface by Louis Budd. $28.50
28. Giovanni Boccaccio, *The Decameron*. English Adaptation by
    Carmelo Gariano. $30.00
29. Giacomo A. Striuli, *"Alienation in Giuseppe Berto"*. $26.50
30. Barbara Mujica, *Iberian Pastoral Characters*. Preface by Fre-
    derick A. de Armas. $33.00
31. Susan Niehoff McCrary, *"'El último godo' and the Dynamics
    of the Urdrama."* Preface by John E. Keller. $27.50
32. *En torno al hombre y a sus monstruos: ensayos críticos sobre
    la novelística de Carlos Rojas*, editados por Cecilia Castro Lee
    y C. Christopher Soufas, Jr. $31.50
33. J. Thomas O'Connell, *Mount Zion Field*. $24.50
34. Francisco Delicado, *Portrait of Lozana: The Lusty Andalusian
    Woman*. Translation, introduction and notes by Bruno M.
    Damiani. $45.50
35. Elizabeth Sullam, *Out of Bounds*. Foreword by Michael G
    Cooke. $23.50
36. Sergio Corsi, *Il "modus digressivus" nella "Divina Comme-
    dia."* $28.75
37. Juan Bautista Avalle-Arce, *Lecturas (Del temprano Renaci-
    miento a Valle Inclán)*. $28.50
38. Rosendo Díaz-Peterson, *Las novelas de Unamuno*. Prólogo
    de Antonio Carreño. $30.00
39. Jeanne Ambrose, *Syntaxe Comparative Français-Anglais*. $29.50
40. Nancy Marino, *La serranilla española: notas para su historia e
    interpretación*. $28.75.
41. Carolyn Kreiter Kurylo, *Contrary Visions*. Preface by Peter
    Klappert. $24.50
42. Giorgio Perissinotto, *Reconquista y literatura medieval: cuatro
    ensayos*. $29.50
43. Rick Wilson, *Between a Rock and a Heart Place*. $25.00
44. *Feminine Concerns in Contemporary Spanish Fiction by
    Women*. Edited by Roberto C. Manteiga, Carolyn Galerstein
    and Kathleen McNerney. $35.00
45. Pierre L. Ullman, *A Contrapuntal Method For Analyzing
    Spanish Literature*. $41.50

46. Richard D. Woods, *Spanish Grammar and Culture Through Proverbs*. $35.00
47. David G. Burton, *The Legend of Bernardo del Carpio. From Chronicle to Drama*. Preface by John Lihani. $30.00
48. Godwin Okebaram Uwah, *Pirandellism and Samuel Beckett's Plays*. $28.00
49. *Italo-Hispanic Literary Relations*, ed. J. Helí Hernández. $33.00
50. *Studies in Honor of Elias Rivers*, eds. Bruno M. Damiani and Ruth El Saffar. $30.00
51. *Discourse Studies in Honor of James L. Kinneavy*, ed. Rosalind J. Gabin. $45.00
52. John Guzzardo, *Textual History and the "Divine Comedy."* $40.50
53. Cheryl Brown Rush, *Circling Home*. Foreword by Sen. Eugene McCarthy. $24.50
54. Melinda Lehrer, *Classical Myth and the "Polifemo" of Góngora*. $39.50
55. Anne Thompson, *The Generation of '98: Intellectual Politicians*. $41.50
56. Salvatore Paterno, *The Liturgical Context of Early European Drama*. Preface by Lawrence Klibbe. $38.50
57. Maria Cecilia Ruiz, *Literatura y política: el "Libro de los estados" y el "Libro de las armas" de Don Juan Manuel*. Prólogo por Diego Catalán. $37.50
58. James P. Gilroy, *Prévost's Mentors: The Master-Pupil Relationship in the Major Novels of the Abbé Prévost*. $39.95
59. *A Critical Edition of Juan Diamante's "La reina María Estuarda,"* by Michael G. Paulson and Tamara Alvarez-Detrell. $44.50
60. David Craig, *Like Taxes: Marching Through Gaul*. Preface by Howard McCord. $21.50
61. M. Cecilia Colombi, *Los refranes en el "Quijote": texto y contexto*. Prólogo por Juan Bautista Avalle-Arce. $40.50
62. *"La mística ciudad de Dios" (1670)*. Edition and Study by Augustine M. Esposito, O.S.A. $36.50
63. Salvatore Calomino, *From Verse to Prose: the Barlaam and Josaphat Legend in 15th Century Germany*. $50.00
64. Gene Fendt, *Works of Love? Reflections on Works of Love*. $37.50
65. Michael Zappala, *Lucian of Samosata in the Two Hesperias: An Essay in Literary and Cultural Translation*. $49.50
66. Oscar Bonifaz, *Remembering Rosario: A Personal Glimpse into the Life and Works of Rosario Castellanos*. Translated and Edited by Myralyn F. Allgood. Prologue by Oscar Bonifaz. Foreword by Edward D. Terry. $27.50
67. *Other Voices: Essays on Italian Regional Culture and Language*. Ed. John Staulo. $35.50
68. Mario Aste, *Grazia Deledda: Ethnic Novelist*. $38.50
69. Edward C. Lynskey, *The Tree Surgeon's Gift*. Foreword by Fred Chappell. $22.50

70. Henry Thurston-Griswold, *El idealismo sintético de Juan Valera*. Prólogo por Lee Fontanella. $44.50

71. Mechthild Cranston, *Laying Ways*. Preface by Germaine Brée. $26.50

72. Roy A. Kerr, *Mario Vargas Llosa: Critical Essays on Characterization*. $43.50

73. Eduardo Urbina, *Principios y fines del "Quijote"*. $45.00

74. Pilar Moyano, *Fernando Villalón: El poeta y su obra*. Prólogo por Luis Monguió. $46.50

75. Diane Hartunian, *La Celestina: A Feminist Reading of the "carpe diem" Theme*. $45.50

76. Victoria Urbano, *Sor Juana Inés de la Cruz: amor, poesía, soledumbre*. Edición y prólogo de Adelaida López de Martínez. $43.50

77. Magda Graniela-Rodríguez, *El papel del lector en la novela mexicana contemporánea: José Emilio Pacheco y Salvador Elizondo*. $46.50

78. Robert L. Sims, *El primer García Márquez: un estudio de su periodismo de 1948-1955*. $48.00

79. Zelda Irene, Brooks, *Poet, Mystic, Modern Hero: Fernando Rielo Pardal*. $49.50

80. *La Celestina*. Edición, introducción y notas de Bruno M. Damiani. $45.00

81. Jean P. Keller, *The Poet's Myth of Fernán González*. $47.50

82. Zelda Irene Brooks, *Carlos Alberto Trujillo: una voz poética de América del sur*. $39.50

83. Maksoud Feghali, *Le phénomène de construction et de destruction dans "Le Songe" de Du Bellay*. Preface by Michael J. Giordano. $49.50

84. Louis Imperiale, *El contexto dramático de La Lozana andaluza"*. Preliminary Note by Bruno M. Damiani. Preface by Marco De Marinis. $49.50

85. Alberto Traldi, *Fascismo y ficción en Italia: cómo los novelistas italianos representaron el régimen de Mussolini*. $49.50

86. Philip Cranston, *Naissances / Births*. $35.00

87. Marjorie Ratcliffe, *Jimena: A Woman in Spanish Literature*. $63.50

88. Víctor Infantes, *En el Siglo de Oro. Estudios y textos de literatura áurea*. $59.50

89. Ofelia L. Alayeto, *Sofía Casanova (1861-1958): Spanish Woman Poet, Journalist and Author*. Preface by Janet Pérez. $54.50

90. María Pilar Celma Valero, *Literatura y periodismo en el fin de siglo 1880-1907*. $85.50

91. María Rubio Martín, *Estructuras imaginarias en la poesía*. $47.50

92. Mercedes Rodríguez Pequeño, *Los formalistas rusos y la teoría de los géneros literarios*. $43.50

93. Gonzalo Corona Marzol, *Aspectos del taller poético de Jaime Gil de Biedma*. $44.70

94. Isabel Paraíso Almansa, *Cómo leer a Juan Ramón Jiménez.* $45.50
95. Rosalía Fernández Cabezón, *Cómo leer a Leandro Fernández de Moratín.* $43.50
96. José Angel Ascunce Arrieta, *Cómo leer a Blas de Otero.* $46.50
97. Alicia H. Puleo, *Cómo leer a Julio Cortázar.* $42.50
98. María Eugenia Lacarra Lanz, *Cómo leer "La Celestina".* $45.50
99. Francisco Garrote Pérez, *Cómo leer el "Lazarillo".* $43.00
100. Juergen Hahn, *Miracles, Duels, and Cide Hamete's Moorish Dissent.* $42.50
101. Mechthild Cranston, *In Language and in Love — Marguerite Duras: The Unspeakable.* $46.75
102. Gerhard Hauck, *Reductionism in Drama and The Theater: The Case of Samuel Beckett.* $59.50
103. Marta Bermúdez Gallegos, *Poesía, sociedad y cultura: diálogos y retratos del Perú colonial.* $49.50
104. *Tractado de vicios e virtudes*: An Edition with Introduction and Glossary by Cleveland Johnson. $49.00
105. Ralph Gunther, *Giants in their Field: An Introduction to the Nobel Prizes in Literature.* $69.50
106. Peggy Whitten Watson, *Intra-historia in Miguel de Unamuno's Novels: A Continual Presence.* $49.50
107. Marianna Merritt Matteson, *Manuel Díaz Rodríguez. Evolution and Dynamics of the Stylist.* $45.00

BOOK ORDERS

* Clothbound. *All book orders,* except library orders, must be prepaid and addressed to **Scripta Humanistica**, 1383 Kersey Lane, Potomac, Maryland 20854. *Manuscripts* to be considered for publication should be sent to the same address.